Have Fun and Get A's

"I definitely wish I read Carolyn's book when I was in college. Her simple step by step process transforms the burden of studying into a fun activity"

—**Rick Frishman**, Publisher Morgan James Publishing

"As a school, we are always concerned about ensuring students have balance in their lives. As Carolyn identifies in this book, it is possible for students to achieve academic excellence and still enjoy life."

—**Kevin McHenry**, Bachelor of Business Administration;
Master of Education, Headmaster of St. Andrew's College

"Carolyn Zhao has really outdone herself with her new book, Have Fun and Get A's. Her insightful journey as a student, university teacher, and parent will enrich the lives of any student facing the struggles of today's competitive education system. This is a book which can definitely inspire many students to be the leaders who can make the world a better place to live"

—**Dr. Jooyon D. Cho**, Principal of
Queen's Collegiate in Ontario, Canada

"This practical, powerful book cuts through the theory and shows you exactly what you can do immediately to get top grades."

—**Brian Tracy**, Thought Leader,
Best Selling Author, Professional Speaker, Entrepreneur

Have Fun and Get A's

HOW TO Study Less
—AND—
Achieve More

CAROLYN ZHAO

New York

Have Fun and Get A's

HOW TO Study Less AND Achieve More

© 2015 CAROLYN ZHAO.

Published in New York, New York, by Morgan James Publishing. Morgan James and The Entrepreneurial Publisher are trademarks of Morgan James, LLC. www.MorganJamesPublishing.com

The Morgan James Speakers Group can bring authors to your live event. For more information or to book an event visit The Morgan James Speakers Group at www.TheMorganJamesSpeakersGroup.com.

bitlit

A **free** eBook edition is available with the purchase of this print book.

CLEARLY PRINT YOUR NAME ABOVE IN UPPER CASE

Instructions to claim your free eBook edition:
1. Download the BitLit app for Android or iOS
2. Write your name in **UPPER CASE** on the line
3. Use the BitLit app to submit a photo
4. Download your eBook to any device

ISBN 978-1-63047-474-4 paperback
ISBN 978-1-63047-475-1 eBook
ISBN 978-1-63047-476-8 hardcover
Library of Congress Control Number:
2014918497

Cover Design by:
Rachel Lopez
www.r2cdesign.com

Interior Design by:
Bonnie Bushman
bonnie@caboodlegraphics.com

In an effort to support local communities and raise awareness and funds, Morgan James Publishing donates a percentage of all book sales for the life of each book to Habitat for Humanity Peninsula and Greater Williamsburg.

Get involved today, visit
www.MorganJamesBuilds.com

Habitat
for Humanity®
Peninsula and
Greater Williamsburg
Building Partner

Have Fun and Get A's

HOW TO Study Less
—AND—
Achieve More

CAROLYN ZHAO

New York

Have Fun and Get A's

HOW TO Study Less AND Achieve More

© 2015 CAROLYN ZHAO.

Published in New York, New York, by Morgan James Publishing. Morgan James and The Entrepreneurial Publisher are trademarks of Morgan James, LLC. www.MorganJamesPublishing.com

The Morgan James Speakers Group can bring authors to your live event. For more information or to book an event visit The Morgan James Speakers Group at www.TheMorganJamesSpeakersGroup.com.

A **free** eBook edition is available with the purchase of this print book.

CLEARLY PRINT YOUR NAME ABOVE IN UPPER CASE

Instructions to claim your free eBook edition:
1. Download the BitLit app for Android or iOS
2. Write your name in **UPPER CASE** on the line
3. Use the BitLit app to submit a photo
4. Download your eBook to any device

ISBN 978-1-63047-474-4 paperback
ISBN 978-1-63047-475-1 eBook
ISBN 978-1-63047-476-8 hardcover
Library of Congress Control Number:
2014918497

Cover Design by:
Rachel Lopez
www.r2cdesign.com

Interior Design by:
Bonnie Bushman
bonnie@caboodlegraphics.com

In an effort to support local communities and raise awareness and funds, Morgan James Publishing donates a percentage of all book sales for the life of each book to Habitat for Humanity Peninsula and Greater Williamsburg.

Get involved today, visit
www.MorganJamesBuilds.com

Habitat
for Humanity®
Peninsula and
Greater Williamsburg
Building Partner

Table of Contents

Foreword

Carolyn Zhao and I met in 2013 in Toronto, but she has been my protégé student in real estate since 2006. As soon as we met, she shared her *amazing* story with me. I was *so* impressed as she told me her story of immigrating to Canada from China. Even though she had been a university professor in China, when she arrived as an immigrant, she had to work at many entry-level sales jobs just to make ends meet. Then she attended one of my real-estate investment seminars in 2006, and through the guidance of my team members, she rose to become a very successful real-estate investor.

However, through the craziness of her daily routines, she didn't lose sight of her main purpose of immigrating to Canada—she wanted her son to have a better education. Her first sign of trouble was when she and her husband were called to the principal's office. "This isn't a good sign," Carolyn thought. And it wasn't a pleasant experience! She made the decision to find the solution to not only her son's education but also the education of students everywhere. And what you'll read in this book is what she discovered.

Like many young people, her son spent many long hours studying. He often studied till midnight or even later to complete his homework. This reminded her of her years as a university professor in China. She witnessed lots of students stare blankly at their homework assignments without knowing how to begin. She sympathized with them, as she too had been through the same struggles. Academic hardships create tons of stress for young people.

She felt responsible to discover new ways to improve the student experience—ways to help students learn faster and even enjoy the process. More importantly, she wanted to help these young students, through their study habits, create healthy and inspirational work habits.

Even though Carolyn uses different terminology in *Have Fun and Get A's*, here's another fun and interesting way she has described the most important "ingredients" for education:

Pragmatic Beans: Pragmatic Beans allow users to connect theories they've learned to solve real-world problems. Today we live in a complex world where our problems overlap many different disciplines. With these beans you will be able to transform the world around you for a better tomorrow. Theory is nothing if it is not put into use. The same can be said for your educational degrees and diplomas. Luckily, the pragmatic beans will help you utilize the information that you have learned and transfer it into practical skills.

Pathos Serum: This serum allows students to interpret other people's feelings based on what they say and how they say it. It will allow you to be better prepared in social interactions to know what others are feeling and how to appropriately respond in order to maintain and build friendship and trust. With this serum, you'll be able to build better connections and influence people.

Learning Tablets: These tablets will give you the power to learn at an exponential rate. With these tablets the ordinary, mundane tasks of studying for a test will become easy and enjoyable. By taking these tablets, you will turn your studying into a fun activity that not only gives you joy, but also stimulates your brain to retain what you have learned longer and more easily. The learning tablets are essential if you want to have fun while learning at the same time.

Spartan Potion: This potion immediately allows you to have complete and total focus. In a world overrun by electronic distractions, it's necessary to have such a potion. This potion gives you the attention span and discipline needed to complete long and tedious tasks. The Spartan Potion works best when combined with the Enjoyment Elixir. This potion will give you a "whatever it takes" attitude that will endure for as long as you are working on your task at hand.

Perseverance Powder: Ingesting this powder allows you to have the mental endurance and strength to face even the toughest challenge. With this powder you will not be hesitant when it comes to commitment. When faced with a challenge, your brain will automatically divide the challenge into manageable portions, so it doesn't seem so daunting. Most importantly, the powder will change your outlook on your failures. Each failure will be now viewed as "feedback."

Strength Syrup: The Strength Syrup increases your bone density by ten times, allowing you to carry a once-thought unimaginable amount of muscle. It also immensely increases your ability to rebuild torn muscle tissue after a workout. And it also increases mental strength. This mental strength can be applied to every facet of life. When faced with a momentous task, or crushed by a debilitating setback, the strength syrup will give you the mental strength and tenacity to get back up and keep on trucking forward.

Enjoyment Elixir: This elixir augments your ability to feel pleasure even in the most barren of situations. Specifically, it increases the flow of dopamine in your body, which is the chemical that gives you pleasure. With this newfound vision of fun and happiness, one can expect to be infinitely more creative. In despair, you will find comfort; in pain, you will find joy; in the face of darkness, you will find light. You will continually aspire to inspire. With this elixir you will be able to find inspiration even in the worst situations. Through this inspiration you will be able fully utilize the talents you have been gifted with and be able to communicate it with the world.

Vision Pills: These pills will give you the necessary attributes to have a strong vision. In our world, we are not surrounded by many who have expansive vision—those who aspire to inspire. We are lacking people who have the courage and wisdom to lead others and to change the world. People are always satisfied with what they have accomplished. With these pills, you will never rest on your laurels. Your mind will not be inhibited by the low standards set by society. Your standards will be sky high. With these pills, you will be ready to serve more people.

Even though Carolyn Zhao is not a specialist in child development, she is able to relate with others through her personal story. By utilizing the tools you'll find in this book, Carolyn converted her son from a weak student into an Ivy League freshman. The process was not pleasant, and was sometimes even harsh, but she did it. She helped him unleash hidden talents and cultivate new characteristics.

You hold in your hands not only a book, but a portal to a new way of education for young people. The purpose of the book is to facilitate a community for such a transformation. Parents and teachers should take on the responsibility of changing our youth into agents of change

rather than victims of it. Young students should take the initiative for the transformation, too. Young people must have the earnest desire to gain their skills and big visions. In the meantime, they shouldn't lose their freedom and fun in their lives. We all need to work together to be a community that inspires betterment and greatness.

Robert G. Allen
#1 New York Times bestselling author
Creating Wealth
Nothing Down
Multiple Streams of Income
The One Minute Millionaire

Acknowledgement

Many thanks to my son Bo for the inspiration to write this book, to my husband John for his ongoing support, and to my mentor Robert G. Allen for his long-term guidance.

And to Rick Frishman, David Hancock, W. Terry Whalin, Margo Toulouse, and all the members of the Morgan James team, and to Amanda Rooker and her editing team at SplitSeed—thank you all for making this book a reality.

Introduction

What Keeps You Studying Until Two A.M.?

It was one-thirty in the morning, and Nancy was helping her son, Bob, study. Bob had been staring at the same homework for at least twenty minutes, with no clue how to solve the problem.

She asked him: "How much more time do you need

to complete your homework? Could you ask someone for help or find any help on the Internet?"

"Could you leave me alone, Mom? I want to take time to complete the work by myself."

Nancy felt helpless. She went to bed. But she suffered, because it hurt her when she saw her son studying until midnight or later every night. Bob felt bad too. But he wanted to try his best to complete his homework perfectly. Sometimes, he discussed it with his classmates. But most times, this did not seem to help. So he decided to find the solution on his own. He believed that he could improve through repetitive studying what he had learned in class. Many homework assignments were very challenging.

In math, for example, the questions were often those that had not been learned. Because he chose the advanced placement course, he was working at a university level. Many questions were beyond what he could handle. In his English course, Bob had to read half the book in one night and rewrite the abstract. In his business class, he was asked to write a complete business plan. He had to access all the data for analyzing the market and the trends, examine the requirements for manufacturing the product, experiment with various electronic hardware, and write a software program to connect the hardware to perform certain functions.

Each course was different, but they all were very challenging for him. He never had enough time for homework. With all of his music and sports activities, he didn't even get home until after six p.m., so it was not hard to understand that he had to study till at least twelve thirty a.m. almost every day.

Every morning, Bob found it very hard to get up. He wished that he could stay in bed, even just for one more minute. That minute of sleep was so sound and sweet. Sometimes, he fell asleep in the middle of class and missed some of the teacher's content. Sometimes, sleeping only five to six hours every day caught up with him, and he got a cold due to his weakened immune system. He felt that being sick would be the worst thing that could happen to him. He was on the varsity football team, and he did not want to lose his muscle and his strength. He wondered how he would balance homework and extracurricular activities.

He wanted to be a good student with high marks, and he wanted to complete each homework assignment with his best effort. Because of his desire for perfection, he was under stress. Bob was a student who was recognized by his teachers for working extremely hard. Did Bob really need to work this hard to get recognition? When Bob was under stress, he was thinking that something was not quite right. But what was it?

Bob is only one example typical of many high school and college students. What other reasons could young students have for staying up late to study? As a university teacher and a parent, I can speculate on a few more.

- Confusion about the material taught in class
- Procrastination
- Excessive use of social media
- Partying or clubbing
- Playing computer games
- Instant messaging
- Mental stress

Out of the many reasons above, the biggest reason for staying up late is stress.

Stress can come from different sources.

First, some students see studying as extremely important. They think that good marks will get them into a good university. If they go to a good university, then they will get a good job. They believe that a good job leads to a decent life. Even if they don't like some of the courses, they still will try their best to get high marks.

Therefore, students are willing to work hard to get higher marks because they believe that good ones will lead to success in the future. That being said, study stress is the number-one stressor for college students.

Second, there is a lot of pressure coming from others, including parents, peers, and teachers. Most of the time, parents put high expectations on their children. Often the students hear stressful nagging—"Have you done your homework?" Moreover, the competition between students creates lots of pressure. Instead of learning at their own pace, students compare their academic performance to others' marks and rankings. The comparison is not helpful, and it creates lots of unnecessary pressure. The students also face expectations from their teachers. The teachers and schools would like them to study hard and gain acceptance to good universities. That's because the teachers want to establish a high-ranking status or reputation for their school.

Third, the stress comes from the students' own belief systems. Another type of student would stay inside the classroom all day and believe that studying hard is the only way to achieve good marks. They give practice and building physical strength less credit. Therefore, they only concentrate on studying and leave no time for fun, sports, and socializing with other students. Their school and personal lives are imbalanced. They study 100 percent of the time, but their brain does not work properly. These factors conspire to render them academically inefficient, and they can easily get stuck.

Fourth, the difference between how students and parents view success also can create stress. This contradiction can develop into strong conflict between them.

How do students see success?

- As having a happy and joyful life
- As enjoying love between themselves and others
- As doing what they are good at and what they love
- As having a good family
- As building good friendships and relationships
- As having a balanced life
- As being healthy physically, mentally, and spiritually
- As placing money second

How do some parents see success?

- As going to good universities
- As studying majors that have higher potential for high incomes
- As having good marks and ranking high in class
- As finding good and stable jobs after college graduation
- As making a good living and being independent
- As having a family and kids

The parents' opinions are practical and result-driven versus the students' journey-focused and happiness-driven views. These different opinions on what constitutes success put students and parents in conflict. In our society, parents try to share what they think is right with their children. Oftentimes, their thoughts are utilitarian and are not what their children want. Parents may try to brainwash their children into believing what they think is right. Parents try to model and teach children based on their past experiences, but in reality, many of their ideas are completely out of touch.

Fifth, students are stressed from the necessity of cramming. Why are they cramming? Most of the time, cramming comes from not planning or not starting early. If the teacher assigns a project that is due in two weeks that means it requires two weeks to complete. But many students think that two weeks is a long time, so they are not in a rush. After a week has passed, they start the project. Then they find out that it needs a lot more work than they expected. Three days before the project is due, they do not know how to complete it. One day before the deadline, they find some mistakes, erase what they have done, and start over again. The night before, they stay up all night to complete the assignment.

The same thing often happens for the exam. Students are given lots of time to review their test material, but do nothing until the night before the exam. Therefore, they have lots of stress and depression.

Because of cramming, students hardly get enough sleep. When that happens,, they create a bad cycle for themselves. The students may experience mood swings, lack of energy during the day, difficulty in concentrating and focusing, and difficulty in receiving, processing, and retaining information. All of these issues can lead to stress.

Sixth, stress can result when students receive destructive criticism from others. Even though students work hard, sometimes they still make mistakes unexpectedly. Parents may see the mistake as a big deal. Because of the criticizing from parents, the students may feel discouraged and guilty right away. The students then fear making mistakes, and eventually, they stop trying. They feel stressed when they don't know how to improve.

Finally, the students feel pressure when adapting to higher course curriculum standards. Courses are getting more complicated and have higher standards each year. Students have to stretch themselves to adapt.

Let us check the news. In a June 2013 story for The Globe and Mail—"Canadian Students Feel Stress, Anxiety, Have Suicidal Thoughts, Survey Reveals"—Adam Miller reported on a survey of more than 30,000 of the country's post-secondary students which showed the following impacts stemming from stressful academic careers:

- Nearly 90 percent of them "felt overwhelmed" during "the past year"
- More than 50 percent "felt hopeless"
- Sixty-three percent "felt very lonely"

Miller also reported the following survey findings about these students: 9. 5 percent had "seriously considered" committing suicide "in the past year," and 1.3 percent reported having "attempted suicide" (www.theglobeandmail.com/news/national/education/college-university-students-feel-stress-anxiety-have-suicidal-thoughts-reveals/article12613742).

Stress is the number-two cause of suicide for college students (accident is the number-one cause).

Another study, from the *Journal of Academics and Business Ethics* in Taiwan (www.aabri.com/manuscripts/10471.pdf), reported on sources of stress. This work, titled "A study of stress sources among college students in Taiwan," was written by Cheng Kai-Wen, who notes: "84.2% of the surveyed adolescents have experienced depression . . . 56.7% of them considered that their depression comes from school stress . . . and 45.6% attributed their depression to academic tests." The survey also revealed that depressed people are eight times more likely to commit suicide than normal people.

More info on the topic comes from reporter Francesca Di Meglio for *Bloomberg Businessweek*. In "Stress Takes Its Toll on College Students," Di Meglio reported in May 2012 for the magazine on the poisonous brew created by high-pressure academic environments, sky-high college tuition, and a slow economy: Already-stressed students, mired in academic debt, graduate into a world where jobs are hard to come by, leading to health problems both mental and emotional.

Di Meglio's article went on to quote the following statistics on college students from a 2012 American College Counseling Association study:

- 37.4 percent who sought help "have severe psychological problems, up from 16 percent in 2000"
- More than 75 percent of 228 counselors "reported an increase in crises in the past five years requiring immediate response"
- Of the 228 counselors, 42 percent saw a spike in self-injury, and 24 percent saw a spike in eating disorders (www.businessweek.com/articles/2012-05-10/stress-takes-its-toll-on-college-students).

From the examples above, we have learned that stress and anxiety are the most prevalent mental health problems that students confront. Clearly, the most successful students are those who best can deal with stress.

From these examples, we also have learned that stress and anxiety are the leading causes of suicide for college students. They take such an extreme action because they think that they cannot deal with their issues anymore.

In the book *How to Win Friends and Influence People,* Dale Carnegie said that success is 5 percent what you know and 95 percent how you relate to people. Carnegie wrote that intelligence is as purchasable a commodity as any other. That means no matter how hard you work on your techniques, you only achieve 5 percent of success. Without a big score in interpersonal skills, the result is a failing grade. If you are a genius, but no one likes you, then your brain is your only commodity.

In reality, many people never use what they learned at school in their work. They learn things on the job. Learning is a lifetime thing. So, if you did not earn good marks in school, it is not the end of the world. You still have lots of time to learn. If the average life expectancy is 80 years old, then you have 960 months, or 29,200 days, or 700,800 hours, or 42,048,000 minutes to learn. You have lots of opportunities.

That said, some university graduates are not good students at all. They do not expect good jobs at the beginning of their careers. They start on what they can where they can. They are not afraid of making mistakes. These students are willing to do very hard work because they do not fear getting their hands dirty. They always get firsthand experience. They only have a few marketable skills, but they work hard to improve them. The experience of having been normal students keeps them humble because they never ascended to the top of the group.

They are flexible and willing to learn new things. They are happy with the small improvements they make each day and look forward to more. Continuous effort and hard work have sharpened their skills and leads them to become experts in their respective fields. They go on to ascend to the top of their industries.

It turns out that many successful people have fewer degrees than unsuccessful people. Why is this? What is the secret behind it? Thomas Edison left school when he was an elementary student. He ended up being homeschooled by his mother. Bill Gates dropped out of university to start his own company. He later created a big philanthropic foundation to help people around the world. Ma Yun said that he wanted to go to a famous university, but he did not have the opportunity to do so. He attended a normal university and changed his career a couple of times before he finally founded the number-one e-commerce company in China, the Alibaba Group.

Chen Yang wrote in *The Global Times,* "The Alibaba Group, which owns China's largest online shopping platforms tmall.com and taobao.com, announced on Tuesday that it had achieved record sales of 35 billion yuan ($5.75 billion) on Monday's Singles' Day, initially created by young people to celebrate their loneliness" (http://www.globaltimes.cn/content/824169.shtml). No other company is even close to beating these sales.

To convince her son to change his attitude toward marks, rankings, and study, Nancy did lots of research. She had no objection to school rankings, but she found that if students pay too much attention to these marks, considering them the only sources to determine whether they are successful, then it can cause lots of stress and negatively influence them. She shared all her research with her son.

"Do you think that there are important qualities other than marks or rankings, Mom?" Bob asked.

"Yes," Nancy answered. "There are some soft qualities that are hidden inside one's personality, but these are hard to quantify, like marks. For example, there's a student's intelligence quotient (IQ), emotional quotient (EQ), or his ability to apply his knowledge and his attitude toward learning, his physical strength, and being well rounded." Bob looked confused, but he thought, *Let's see.* Keep on reading.

Chapter 1

IQ and EQ

Twenty years ago, society was simple. There was discipline and authority. Even if they had a low emotional quotient (EQ), people were fine as long as they had a high intelligence quotient (IQ).

What is IQ?

The intelligence quotient is a score derived from one of several standardized tests designed to assess and evaluate intelligence.

People used to think that as long as they were good at math, physics, and chemistry, they would have no problem finding a job. Nowadays, if you are only good at math, physics, and chemistry, you may have a hard time finding a job. There is not much correlation between marks and jobs. Society has become complicated. If you only pay attention to IQ, you will find it hard to adapt to our new world.

In 1983, Harvard psychologist Howard Gardner, in his book *Frames of Mind,* proposed the Theory of Multiple Intelligences. Gardner articulated seven criteria of behavior to be considered intelligence.

In 1991, psychologist Peter Salovey, who is now president of Yale University, and J. D. Mayer first introduced the concept of the emotional quotient.

In 1995, then *New York Times* writer Daniel Goleman published *Emotional Intelligence,* a book that brought a new wave of thinking into America and the whole world.

What is EQ?

The concept of emotional intelligence is a revolution in the field of human intelligence. Emotional intelligence is the ability to perceive emotions, the ability to harness emotions and facilitate critical thinking and problem solving, the ability to understand and appreciate emotions, the ability to control one's own emotions, and the ability to recognize other's feelings so that you can move people to desired emotional levels.

Nowadays, young people not only are required to have a high IQ, but also to have a high EQ.

In other words, not only are you required to know how to study, but also to understand the emotional environment that you are situated in, respond to that situation, and adapt yourself to any changes. If a student only knows how to study and achieve high marks, but lacks the influence of peers, leadership skills, empathy, or community interest, then he/she is less likely to be successful in the future.

To be successful, you need 80 percent EQ and 20 percent IQ.

20% IQ + 80% EQ = 100% success

Understanding the Emotional Intelligence Theory can improve your EQ index greatly. This, in turn, will help you obtain intangible benefits for your life and career.

Nancy was out of town on a business trip. Her son called her. "Mom, I need some help here." "What has happened?" she asked cautiously, as she thought that there might be an emergency. He answered, "You know, I have five projects to complete this month, and I am very nervous. I think that you may need to come back and help me." "What are the five projects?" Nancy asked. He said, "We are going to Harry Rosen to present our marketing strategies to help improve their sales next Wednesday. Afterward, we need to stay in Toronto and perform in MusicFest nationals. Next, our French presentation on a French invention is due on Friday. We have an English project too. We have an AP math exam. Everything is this month, and it is crazy. I just feel that I cannot breathe, Mom."

Nancy thought, *Oh, boy, my poor baby, too much work.* But she told him, "Relax, you can do this by yourself. I trust you. I will help you. But, first, let's analyze it together.

"For the Harry Rosen presentation, you and your team members have worked together for a few weeks already. Your group has developed a marketing plan. It is a team project, so do your part, and remember you have other team members supporting you as well. Plus, you have already had several group discussions. I think that you are prepared. Keep communicating with your team members and update your marketing plan regularly. But please don't try to be perfect. You need to go and present your plan, and then you will get feedback from Harry Rosen.

"For the music performance, you have practiced twice a week for three continuous months. You were prepared a long time ago. Just put on your music tie, wear your kilt and your school uniform, and present yourself.

"Also, for the performance and the presentation, you will never be fully prepared until you perform in front of the audience. Keep a clear mind, a positive attitude, and a passionate heart; you will bring your positive energy to the audience. It is very important to fully understand your material—the music piece, the author, the historical background, and the big 'why' behind the piece. For example, in your music performance, your goal is to convey the 'why' to the audience, to deliver the composer's passion. How much you know the material and how well you perform the content make you a good performer. But how you deliver the author's passion and how you make the audience feel make you a great performer. How can you prepare that? Be relaxed and have a fun time. Fifty percent of the time, you prepare the material; 50 percent of the time, you need to use your creativity and talent to serve other people. That is called improvisation. You need to have a good night's sleep, keep a fresh memory, and be ready to fire up your passion.

"For the other projects and assignments, just take some time to prepare. If you don't know how, then you can ask your teacher for help, discuss it with friends, or search the Internet. Today, anyone can find almost anything on the Internet. You need to find the material you need and write your own assignment. Please ask me if you don't know how.

"Lastly, you cannot pursue perfection, simply because perfection does not exist. Just do it. Consider that you have already had version one, which is better than version none. Don't you agree? You can always go back and update version one to version two as the project goes along. As the famous Internet marketing expert Alex Mandossian said, 'Sloppy success is better than perfect mediocrity.'

"Another very important thing: No matter how hard you work, you cannot prepare everything. You just cannot. There is a plan; there is also change. You need to change yourself right away to adapt to that change. Art Linkletter said, 'If you want to make God laugh, tell him your plans.' You need to be creative. But I believe that you can do it.

"There are so many high school students and university students under stress because of heavy loads of assignments and homework. You should be aware that you are primarily learning *the ability to study, not the material.* Only a small percentage of what you learn will be used at work if you are lucky; the rest will likely never be used in your lifetime. Learning is a lifetime activity.

"Back in May 2013, I heard the successful real estate investor and educator Robert Allen say in a seminar in Toronto, 'To be successful, you need 15 percent of V-How, 20 percent of We-How, and 65 percent of Be-How.' V-How is the knowledge and vehicle that you choose to focus on to be successful. We-How is the team that you work with to reach your goal. Be-How is the mental attitude or disposition that predetermines a person's responses to and interpretations of situations. It is how you think. It is called mindset."

Once Nancy shared these ideas with her son, he asked, "Why do we need to study so hard for these things if we only use a little bit of it to become successful?" Nancy responded, "Right, so just relax. School study improves your learning skills and learning ability, and most importantly helps you create good working habits for your lifetime. Once you have good learning abilities and work habits, you can adapt to the new world in the future."

"Oh," her son murmured. Nancy said, "Try your best to accomplish great schoolwork. If you make mistakes, it is not the end of the world. Make a mistake, correct it, and study again. It is okay if your work is not perfect or you are not the best in the class or school." "Thank you, Mom. I really appreciate what you said. I thought that you would want me to study very hard, study every minute, pursue becoming number one, and have no fun."

"You misunderstood me, baby," said Nancy. "I always wish you the very best and want you to try your best. But there is only one best or number one in your class. If you are not the number-one student, I am fine with that. I would accept it. I really appreciate the efforts that you put into your work. I praise you based on your efforts, not just your results. As long as you try your best, I am very happy. I am so proud of the progress that you have made through your work. I think that effort is more important than results."

Nancy continued, "Mom wants you to have some playtime too. Create a balanced life. Have fun and get A's."

Bob started to think of his mother in a strange way. For so many years, he had misunderstood her. Suddenly he felt that she understood him, and he felt close to her.

Many young people see university as their only gateway to a successful life. They see that big companies often hire good students from universities even before they graduate. Those companies offer good salaries. So students try hard to get good marks.

Nancy's friend's son Jason had been a student in the gifted class since grade one, and the number-one student there to boot. Not only did he get good marks, but he also had talent in various extracurricular activities. He had played piano very well since the age of five, competing in several national competitions in Canada and even winning a few times. He also was a figure skater and a great tennis player. Before graduating from high school, he received several offers from top universities. His top two were Harvard and the University of Waterloo. He did not know which one he should choose. He asked his parents. They said, "Let's see which one will give you a better future."

At Harvard, Jason would study various subjects in the arts and sciences, but his degree would not indicate the type of job that he would get in the future. At the University of Waterloo, Jason would study applied math, which was the best major at that school.

His parents did some research and found out that some students who graduated with a degree in applied math got positions at Google and Facebook. Their salaries jumped to $200,000 within two years, and they were involved in interesting projects. Without asking Jason about his preference, his parents said to him, "Look, going to Harvard

University is like going to high school; you don't have a major in your area of focus. You will learn a little bit of everything. But if you go to Waterloo, you will get a good job with a high salary. We think that you should choose Waterloo." Jason was a good boy who listened to his parents, so he chose the University of Waterloo.

Nancy thought that if she were Jason's mother, she would have let her son decide which university he would attend. She also wanted to encourage her son to study broadly at first, not focus on a certain subject. With the world changing so rapidly, it is good for students to study multidisciplinary or interdisciplinary fields to learn to adapt to new jobs. Students need a breadth of knowledge. What do I mean by breadth of knowledge?

Let me illustrate with an example. Below is what happened to BlackBerry Limited, according to an Associated Press report that appeared in the *Toronto Star* on September 20, 2013.

According to the article, BlackBerry reported it would lay off 40 percent of its global workforce—news that came in the wake of BlackBerry, at one time the "most valuable company" in Canada, self-reporting a nearly $1 billion second-quarter loss. Since  June 2008, the article said, the company's stock had nosedived from more than $140 a share "to less than $9" (http://www.thestar.com/business/2013/09/20/blackberry_shares_halted_pending_news.html).

Think about this: If you are a top engineer at RIM, and you are laid off, what are you going to do? One of my friends held a senior position at Texas Instruments ten years ago, but he was laid off. He had to start over from scratch, just like a student fresh out of college.

The world has changed. In our parents' time, once they had a job, they kept it for life. It was secure. When they retired, they got good benefits from a pension plan. Now, as a university/college graduate, you may not find a job. Even if you do find one, it is not for a lifetime. You need to create everything from scratch and not expect too much from society. You need to be sharp! So, you need a breadth of knowledge—in other words, an understanding of two or more subjects. For example, suppose you want to become an electrical engineer. I encourage you to study not only electrical engineering (one subject), but also mechanical engineering (mixing two subjects) or mining (blending the subject with an industry). A wide range of mixing and blending your studies will give you a wide range of career choices.

So, if you are prepared for the future and the company you work for is not going well, then you have more to offer to other companies or other industries. Breadth of knowledge gives you peace of mind.

Many universities are encouraging students to choose courses from different colleges. For example, the University of Pennsylvania offers coordinated dual degrees and accelerated degrees. One hundred percent of their students are taking courses from two different colleges. Brown University offers academic buffets to students. It does not matter which major you pick; you are allowed to choose different courses that interest you most. Upon completing a certain number of credits, you are ready to graduate. Yale University encourages their students to choose courses that may have nothing to do with their subject major.

You must master a breadth of knowledge to adapt to world change.

Timing is important. The types of jobs that graduates get depend upon the time they graduate. A single individual cannot predict how the world is going to change. Just like Malcolm Gladwell's book *Outliers* says, most computer experts were born between 1950 and 1955. When computer technology was thriving around 1975, these experts were about twenty-five years old and had already started their careers.

If it is a hot career now, it may not be a hot career four years from now. That is why it is important to prepare yourself as a young graduate. You cannot predict the trend, but you can prepare yourself to catch the wave.

Nancy told her son that young students prepare themselves to adapt to big changes. As long as you have prepared yourself, it doesn't matter how the world is changing. You have the ability to adapt.

It is the same as playing basketball. In a basketball game, everyone needs to stay in his or her own position. When the game starts, everyone does his or her own job. Whether offense, defense, running the ball, or passing it to others, they work together as a team to win. If everyone is chasing the ball, then no one sticks to his own position; it is less likely that they will win.

Do you think that Jason will get as good a job as he expects after graduation? No one can predict this because the world is changing every day.

Let's say that you went to a good university and got a good job after graduation. Congratulations!

If you didn't, it is okay. Congratulations too! Why? Because it is not the end of the world. Even if you didn't go to a good university or didn't get a good job, you can still have lots of opportunities. Not attending your ideal university does not stop the progress of your study.

Not having your dream job will take you along a different route than you planned, but that does not mean that you have failed. It means that you will have a better way to use your talent. You are still progressing forward. You did not fail at anything, and you did not miss anything.

What if you are a university graduate, but do not find a job for a long time? Don't worry. Keep looking for a job or create your own and become self-employed. There is always something you can do.

Twenty to thirty years ago, almost every university graduate was guaranteed a job, but now many university students cannot find employment. The traditional industry has changed; many people have become self-employed. Employees are now becoming contractors. There are not many permanent positions out there. There are no guarantees in the world.

Even though employees become contractors, the work they are doing is not called a "job" anymore. However, both employees and employers are very happy. An employer does not have to pay big money to the government for employment insurance and taxes. If the economy is under pressure and the employer doesn't have enough work, then the employer can simply say no to his or her self-employed contractors without offering a big severance package.

The employees are very happy too. Once they become self-employed, they will receive more net income, even though their employer still pays them the same amount of money, and they can claim some bills as business expenses. For both employer and employee, it is a win-win situation. The world is changing. There will be more and more people self-employed. So don't even imagine that the world will provide you a decent job and offer you a big salary after you graduate. You need to create your own job. So relax, because a degree certificate does not equal a job.

Nancy kept sharing these kinds of ideas with her son. But after listening to what she said, Bob asked her a surprising question.

"Mom, can I not go to university?"

"No, you have to go. Only if you have a big idea that you want to implement right away will I support you not going to university. Otherwise, you still have to go and get the education and meet likeminded friends. Don't think that you could be Bill Gates if you don't go to university. That kind of thinking is a little bit odd. Keep doing what you are doing now, start where you can start now, and constantly note the problems that you see in society. Find the solution for those problems, and share it with the community."

Bob was astonished. It was the first time that he had had such a thoughtful, deep conversation with his mother. He liked what she had said. It had made complete sense. He started to think about preparing for higher education and the multidisciplinary and interdisciplinary type of study it would involve. He thought that his mother was going to talk about marks, outcomes, standards, or competency—that she was going to be "old-school style." Now, instead, he felt that his mother understood him even more. *Thanks, Mom,* he thought.

Chapter 2

Mind and Hand

On a quiet summer night around two a.m., cars travel over a bridge, their occupants were oblivious to a man standing on top of it preparing to jump. A light wind rushes over him as he ignores the car fumes, and he smiles wanly as he recalls a few sweet memories. The son of a school principal, he was born in a small town and grew up in a decent family. He received the highest score on his school's university admission test and went on to attend a prestigious university. He married and had a son and daughter. His family life was idyllic. He was close to his wife and children.

Then the man remembered how he had worked hard to earn his double doctoral degrees. With ambition and passion, he had sent out résumés to different companies. He wanted to get a good job, make a decent income, and support his family, but he wasn't any having luck achieving any of that. Some company managers said that he was overqualified; some said that his qualifications did not match the position he was applying for; and others said that they simply were not hiring.

Today's society is so unfair! he thought. After all his studying and the many sleepless nights he endured to earn his double degrees, how could these companies not appreciate his talents and education? *Why can't I get hired?* he wondered. He knew that he had great value to offer many companies, but his continual state of unemployment had thrown him into a deep depression. Now he was standing on the top of the bridge, contemplating ending his life. He felt strongly that if he committed a publicized suicide, it would wake up the type of company managers who had not hired him and would shake up society in general.

As he closed his eyes, a light wind kissed his face. "I devote myself to waking up society," he said, and then jumped into the spiraling waters below. The local news reporters announced his death the same day. Many viewers saw the report and wondered why the man killed himself.

Sadly, many people today find themselves with degrees and no jobs. In recent years, university graduates have flooded the job market, but only a few are hired for jobs they want. Many of those who cannot gain employment turn to self-employment. Or if a graduate is fortunate enough to find a job, many times they are not paid well. For instance, the cost of education is now 20 percent higher than it was ten years ago and university graduates with an applied arts degree earn 12 percent less than high school graduates (once their education costs are factored in).

Sears president Julius Rosenwald suggested: "If you have a lemon, make lemonade."

What do these facts tell us? Studying hard is important, but the application of knowledge is even more important. However, what you are studying must solve a real problem in the real world. If your subject matter is solving a real life problem, how can you not find a job?

In an interview, an employer will assess whether you are a good fit for the job he or she is offering. What does "fit" mean? "Fit" involves the advancement, development, and practical application of science or arts in connection with real-life needs or real-life problems. The needs and problems might be scientific or industrial; they also could be social, artistic, humanistic, and so on. Through the fit, the matches between employers and employees are established and the job is created. John Dewey, the modern father of education, pointed out that learning and application are equally important. In 1902, he stated in his classic book, *The Child and the Curriculum*, "The child is simply the immature being who is to be matured; he is the superficial being who is to be deepened." It is through the practice and the application of learned knowledge that students are deepened.

In Dewey's book *Democracy and Education*, he also pointed out that "if knowledge comes from the impressions made upon us by natural objects, it is impossible to procure knowledge without the use of objects which impress the mind." This means we must practice what we have learned in order to let the knowledge print a deep mark on us. The more we use it, the deeper an impression the knowledge makes on us.

Knowledge is artificial and degrees are superficial without applying knowledge in the real world.

It is through the application and practice of knowledge that students gradually understand the theory and nature of objects. Through the practice, they also gradually come to understand the relationship between humans and objects and the idea of humans as practitioners. None of this type of knowledge can be acquired apart from activity in application and production. None of this type of knowledge can be obtained inside the classroom. None of this type of knowledge can be deepened without practice.

Knowledge, according to the cherished academic tradition, was to be pursued for its own sake with personal interest, not as a necessary preparation for a useful profession.

The journal *Transactions of the American Philosophical Society* says, "Knowledge is of little use, when confined to mere speculation: But when speculative truths are reduced to practice, when theories, grounded upon experiments, are applied to the common purposes of life; and when, by these, agriculture is improved, trade enlarged, the arts of living made more easy and comfortable, and of course, the increase and happiness of mankind promoted; knowledge then becomes really useful. That this Society, therefore, may, in some degree, answer the ends of its institution, the members propose to confine their disquisitions, principally, to such subjects as tend to the improvement of their country, and advancement of its interest and prosperity."

Knowledge without application is useless—it remains theoretical and superficial. According to Massachusetts Institute of Technology founder, William Barton Rogers, the advance of scientific knowledge can be achieved only through a disposition to seek out and explore new paths through experiment and unbiased observation (*Mind and Hand: The Birth of MIT*). Knowledge is only the understanding; it is the application that brings the knowledge to a useful end.

Don't mistake the knowledge for the product. Also don't mix the degree with the real professions or jobs.

The famous British philosopher and thinker Francis Bacon said, "Knowledge is power!" Normally, people think that if you learn history, you will be wise; if you read poetry, then you will be intelligent; if you know calculus, then you will be precise; if you understand philosophy, then you will be profound; if you learn ethics, then you will have accomplishment; and if you study logic, then you will learn how to debate.

In Chinese words, it is written like: 读史使人明智，读诗使人聪慧，演算使人精密，哲理使人深刻，伦理学使人有修养，逻辑修辞使人善辩。

But in reality, knowledge is not power. It is only a personal preference of learning for its own sake.

Knowledge only becomes powerful when it is put into production. With the help of knowledge, new graduates learn to master their environment and improve life on earth.. Only when graduates use knowledge to change the world do they become engineers, artists, or social servants.

Chairman Mao Zedong said, "If you have the wrong mentality, the more knowledge you have, the worse you become." 毛说： "思想及路线错了，知识越多越反动." Though this message was conveyed in a negative way, there is some truth in it. This message is similar to how Americans advanced the Enlightenment (the movement promoting reason and individualism) in the eighteenth century after the Industrial Revolution in Europe. The Enlightenment was first brought to Europe, but Americans practiced the spirit of the Enlightenment repetitively and made the American economy thrive in a short period of time.

Knowledge is understanding. Only if students put their practice into action, ground their knowledge into experiments again and again, and apply their knowledge to a common purpose of life and industry, will they gain useful knowledge. The practice and application adapt the industrial and social needs, revolutionize the environment, enlarge the arts of living, and increase the happiness of mankind. The knowledge becomes really useful.

In modern society, we are facing another industrial revolution, which is happening now. As a commercial realtor (as well as a teacher), I have recognized that there are many vacant office buildings . . . and there are going to be more vacancies. Why? Computer technology, Internet technology, and Wi-Fi frequency have become more advanced.

Traditionally, an employer needs lots of employees in the office. Not anymore. Employers can hire a virtual assistant to complete many tasks for much less money. QQ, Facebook, WeChat, and Google make life easier. As long as you have the Internet, you can call other people all over the world. You don't have to go to a physical "office" to meet your employees. Many things can be virtual now. Shopping is virtual. If you can click the mouse to go to taobao.com, and the third-party escrow service Alipay receives the payment and delivers your clothes to your door, then why should you go to a retail store? There are many new things coming to the world every day. New technology challenges traditional industry. For example, Ma Yun said in one of his presentations that whoever has the widest ranging Wi-Fi will own the customer database. So some businesses are prosperous today, but they may be wiped out in the next few years. Computers and the Internet have changed the world. The second industrial revolution is going on right now. It is called the e-revolution.

This e-revolution brings a lot of change for traditional industry. That is why we cannot stay inside the classroom, just learn theory and neglect practice. Only through practice can we adjust our learning to be realistic and useful.

Shopping

Traditionally, people used to go to a retail store to buy clothes, shoes, bags, and furniture for families. On September 3, 1995, eBay was born in San Jose, California. On May 10, 2003, Taobao was born in China. As of March 31, 2013, there were 760 million products listed on Taobao. People can buy clothes, beds, gifts online, and get 30 percent off the regular price. Moreover, everything you buy is sent to your door. Once you have received the product and decided that you are happy with it, then you confirm the payment with the deliveryman. If people can obtain this type of service online, then why would they drive a car or take a bus to go to the physical retail store? In recent years, there have been lots of vacancies in plazas and shopping malls, and it is not hard to understand why. On November 11, 2013, Alibaba Group, the owner of China's largest online shopping centers tmall.com and taobao.com, announced that it had achieved a daily sales record of 35 billion RMB. That day was created by young people to celebrate their loneliness (http://www.globaltimes.cn/content/824169.shtml).

It is impossible for any retail store to sell $1 billion worth of revenue in one day when you consider that $10 billion in gross sales is closer to what a good brick-and-mortar company makes in one year.

Without endlessly testing markets, it is hard to find market trends and drive high sales worldwide.

Company size and employees

Traditionally, company size and success is measured by a firm's number of employees. To retain employees, you need to pay them a salary, benefits, and provide them with office space. If you had a thousand employees, people used to assume that your company must be very big and admirable. Now, however, that is not the case. The employers, no matter how big or small the company, try to save overhead expenses by reducing costs. For instance, they can hire a virtual assistant who could literally live in another country. A virtual assistant is always much cheaper than an onsite employee. Employers don't have to provide a desk and office for them. They can work comfortably in their own home. The employers can send instructions to these assistants through email, text, or telephone. With the convenience of social media, they can conduct their company meetings virtually. There are many social media platforms worldwide: Google+, GoToMeeting, Facebook, LinkedIn, Twitter, WeChat, QQ, Weibo, HootSuite, and much more. With Google+, you can have up to one hundred people meeting at the same time. You can only have ten people on video, but

you can choose anyone to speak on the video. Meeting online saves lots of time and travel.

Without practicing the use of social media, it is not easy to determine the market trends that result from relying more and more on the virtual world. However, if you worked in any of the industries listed above, you would probably already understand that there are fewer needs for office buildings and retail plazas. Firsthand practice is the best teacher.

Bookstores, coffee shops, trains, airports, and bus station waiting areas

In September 2013, I planned to go to LA. Sitting in the Toronto airport, I was amused. There was an iPad connected to Wi-Fi in front of each seat in the coffee shop. If you wanted to go online, check your email, or do some business, you were welcome to do so. Many patrons filled this coffee shop. That said, the coffee shop that did not have this type of service was half-empty.

The bookstore also is changing. Many people buy books from Amazon instead of the bookstore. They can read on digital devices like a Kindle instead of on paper. Amazon is the number-one online bookstore. People can save 30 to 50 percent on book purchases when they buy their books online. Why? Because there is no printing cost. I used to think that reading a book on my computer might disturb my eyes. After I downloaded a Kindle app, I was amazed. Kindle just has the right lighting and text size for me to read; I can read faster on my Kindle than I can read a paper book.

The company that has wide-ranging Wi-Fi will be the big winner in the future, simply because it has the largest client database.

The invention of social media has reduced the amount of time we spend on the phone. Many people around the world use Skype for business communication for free. Now we have the convenience of WeChat. Facebook is another convenient communication tool. As long as we have Wi-Fi, communication will be no problem. Importance used to be placed on how big a company's phone plan was; now, Internet-based communication significantly reduces the need for phone minutes. Even though the mobile company gives you the minutes for free, you don't need them; you only need the gigabytes. Many people are available on social media or email at any time, but not on the phone. Therefore, social media allows you to complete what you need to do.

High-tech companies

These days, high-tech companies are taking over other companies constantly. New high-tech companies are created every day, along with young billionaires like Facebook owner Mark Zuckerberg and Dropbox owner Drew Houston. Some companies, like Nortel and BlackBerry, have been wiped out because they did not adapt to the changes. There are news things coming to the world. We need to acclimate.

Commercial real estate

Commercial real estate faces lots of challenges. Many small businesses are out of the game. People buy online and get much cheaper stuff, either new or used. A brick-and-mortar company cannot compete with online companies. The cost for online products is low. Online businesses don't require office space or on-site employees; therefore, they can always offer the lowest price. That said, many retail stores are now empty. Employers have reduced their square footage use year by year. Once their lease is up, employers often choose to reduce their square footage by half. I am friends with a lawyer whose law firm is very big. His firm used to lease three floors at a major intersection in uptown Toronto. Its lease was due the summer of 2013, and so the firm downsized its office to one floor. The office space is downsized, but the business has grown almost three times during the last five years.

New industry revolution—e-revolution—needs new actions. That is the application and practice. Just like Americans advanced the Enlightenment, e-revolution needs people to recognize this revolution and use their knowledge and put it into practice.

We are not here to discourage students from gaining knowledge. We want them to understand that knowledge remains largely artificial and superficial without real world engagement. Without practicing, they will less likely understand the market trends, the products, and the services. They cannot understand the relationship between the three. They don't have an idea how to cooperate with others either. Therefore, if students only study hard and pursue high marks, they may receive lots of good grades, but they won't help later in business.

"思想及路线错了，知识越多越反动。" Mao Zedong's words bear repeating: The more knowledge you have, the worse you become if you have the wrong mentality. In other words, people are less likely to take action if they study too much. The more they study, the more confused they become, and knowledge without practice creates more confusion. They don't know where and how to start practicing. Author Robert G. Allen wrote in the book *Cash in a Flash*, "Knowledge is addictive. Often the more you know, the more you think you need to know in order to get started." People always think, *We will practice that when we do comprehensive research and know everything.* When are they going to know everything? That time never comes. It is impossible to know everything before you can practice what you have learned. Practicing brings a deeper understanding to what you have studied. Therefore, with practice, an individual can have a stronger grasp of the subject matter they have learned through books.

Isaac Newton and John Locke helped launch the Enlightenment in Europe and gave it respectability. Then Americans embraced the principles of the Enlightenment, wrote them into law, crystallized them into institutions, and put them to work. That is how America prospered from nothing. Mao Zedong also said: "理论联系实践."("Theory connects practice.") "实践出真知." ("Practice produces truth.")

Years ago, Nancy, the mother who we introduced to you at the start of this book, worked in a university. There was an old story told around campus: A professor in the civil engineering department taught the students how to design buildings. Every student listened carefully and learned. After the class, the professor asked each student to design a small project. It could be a bedroom, kitchen, washroom, school, library, etc.

A young man named Tony was the top student in the class. He designed his project really small and simple. He wanted to design a washroom for a school playground. First he went to the playground to measure the washroom there, then he set about designing his own washroom. In his design there were fancy lights, high-end toilet seats, and granite sinks. In each separate toilet room, he designed nice doors with cute knobs. After he submitted his assignment to the professor, the professor lifted his eyebrows. *What happened?* the professor wondered in disappointment. Why was the professor dissatisfied? Because the student designed a perfect washroom for a playground, but without an entry door. What a hilarious mistake! From that moment on, the professor instituted a policy for the whole department: For any design assignment, students were not only required to design on paper but also to build a real mini-model using the material the students chose. The professor told the students that any design without a real model was not called designing, but dreaming.

In science and technology, we have too many brilliant people who have great ideas but live in theoretical worlds inside their brains. If they are asked to solve real-life problems using their knowledge, they do not have a clue. They don't know how to apply it. They have no idea what is behind the theories. They become frustrated, because their knowledge has become useless.

We must combine the mind and the hand—learn the knowledge and apply the knowledge.

The same thing applies to universities that offer social science programs. If you study a business program, you have learned all types of business concepts; however, you also must apply them in the real world. Many students can write a perfect business plan. They know what type of products and services they provide for their customers. They also have a clear understanding of their target audience, including geographically and physiologically. They have both a primary and secondary target audience. They understand how to describe their products and services in business images, features, and benefits. They are creative enough to invent their logos, titles, and marketing plans. They also are widely aware of their unique selling propositions. They can tell a story about their products and services, sometimes even animating the story. They carefully design their marketing campaign. They plan to keep their customers happy with their products and services, adding value if there are concerns about the price. They are thinking about their partners and establishing referral programs. But as a matter of fact, they never even do these things. A perfect plan without execution is nothing. If it does not work, why do you bother to write the business plan? The entire plan must be written and applied gradually. Strike out the things that are not working and leave the things that are working, then update your business plan regularly.

This principle is applied to art students as well. The only way that they can deepen their knowledge is to practice it more and more. The more they practice it, the more they share their work, the better their work becomes, and the more successful they become.

For example, the Varsity Show, founded in 1894, is one of the oldest traditions at Columbia University, and certainly its oldest performing arts tradition. Composers, writers, and performers are recognized in the Varsity Show, such as Oscar Hammerstein II (class of 1916) and Richard Rodgers (class of 1923). Each year, the Varsity Show attracts some of Columbia and Barnard college's finest actors and creative talents. Many times these students ascend to Broadway. Many of them band together to collaborate. Their ongoing efforts have made many of them very famous. They provide the most entertaining shows in the world because they perform over and over again. Practice makes perfect.

Rodgers started to work with Hammerstein as a freshman. In 1957, Rodgers and Hammerstein's musical masterpiece *Cinderella* appeared on television, with music by Rodgers and book and lyrics by Hammerstein. The story is based on the French version *Cendrillon, ou La Petite Pantoufle de Verre,* by Charles Perrault. Cinderella was forced into servitude by her cruel stepmother and self-centered stepsisters, but she dreamed of a better life. With the help of her Fairy Godmother, she was transformed into a princess.

Cinderella is the only Rodgers and Hammerstein musical written for television. It was originally broadcast live on CBS on March 31, 1957, as a vehicle for Julie Andrews, who played the title role. The broadcast was viewed by more than 100 million people. It subsequently was remade for television twice, in 1965 and 1997.

The musical also has been adapted for the stage in a number of different versions, including a London West End pantomime adaptation, a New York City Opera production that follows the original television version closely, and several touring productions. A 2013 adaptation starring Laura Osnes and Santino Fontana, with a new book by Douglas Carter Beane, opened in 2013 on Broadway. This production is expected to begin a national tour in the 2014–2015 season.

It is the continual remaking of this musical that has improved it over the years; again, practice makes perfect.

Dropbox

Dropbox is a file-hosting service that offers cloud storage, file synchronization, and client software. It was founded in 2007 by Drew Houston, who was mentioned earlier in this chapter, and Arash Ferdowsi. In November 2013, Dropbox reached 200 million users, for both personal and business needs. It also has started to design newer versions of its apps for IOS.

Houston developed the idea when he studied at MIT. He repeatedly forgot his USB flash drive for his files. So he started to wonder how he could store his files somewhere that would not require the flash drive. He said that existing services at the time "suffered problems with Internet latency, large files, bugs, or just made me think too much" (http:// en.wikipedia.org/wiki/Dropbox_(service)).

He was inspired by the way his campus network was set up and invented the file sharing site to track document changes and stay organized without a flash drive. He made something for his personal use. Then he realized that other people may have the same problems. Houston founded Dropbox as his solution to that peeve. According to *Forbes,* Houston has a personal net worth of $ 1.2 billion. His company Y Combinator's most successful investment to date is said to be valued at up to $10 billion. It was not the theory, but his application of his knowledge that made him a successful man.

EdX

EdX is a massive open online course platform designed by MIT and Harvard University in May 2012. The main focus is to provide students with university-level courses for free. It also is very useful for people who conduct research for learning. Currently, it has 1.2 million users.

Universities around the world offer courses through edX. EdX has engaged in a number of partnerships with educational institutions in the United States, China, Mongolia, and India, creating courses in "flipped classrooms" (virtual classrooms).

With its identity in online learning and distance education, edX provides very practical courses through data and videos. All its data are collected through the universities' courses.

EdX offers flipped classrooms with hybrid or blended learning models with interactive components. Each week, a new learning sequence is released in an edX course. The learning sequence is composed of short videos interspersed with active learning exercises. Through the platform and its interactive experience, the students can immediately practice the concepts from the videos and design their own real system if they need to.

Here is a quiz. If you have an idea for how to solve a real-life problem, what are you going to do with it?

A. Share it
B. Write it
C. Tell Mom
D. Just do it

I hope that you chose D.

It is very important to learn things by mind and apply things by hand. The student first gains knowledge by studying inside the classroom and then takes that knowledge outside the classroom to put it into practice. From the application of ideas, he or she will have a deeper understanding of the knowledge. From there, they can form a higher level of theory. They are consistently improving their results by going from mind to hand again, from hand to mind again. The more they repeat the process, the better the results they will create.

Learning things by practicing, or by "hand," is the most important way to improve your intellectual capacity. Just do it, by hand. "Do" is a big part of intellectual achievement.

vMind without hand is useless. Hand without mind is dangerous.

Education is not about marks. There are lots of marks to receive, but they won't help.

The process keeps repeating. Without mind to hand, high marks are superficial. Deeper understanding comes by hand, by practice.

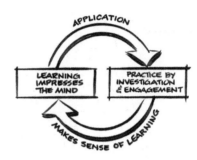

Therefore, a problem-based learning activity or inquiry-based learning is widely used in our modern society.

Nancy shared the mind and hand theory with her son, and he looked confused. She asked him to think about twenty adults he knew of. Out of those twenty adults, she asked him how many he thought were successful. He said that he thought about one or two of them were. Nancy asked him to describe the common characteristics of these two people. He thought and thought, and he decided the commonality was that they used little-known knowledge and practiced day and night crazily. They never feared getting their hands dirty. He started to think more about the mindset that successful people had. He began to discover that mind and hand was in fact one of the secrets of successful people.

Chapter 3

Activity-Based Learning

ost of us have observed that kindergarten students can only stay focused for five minutes if they are put inside a classroom. After that, they become distracted and start to wander. But if the same group is on the playground, they can stay focused for hours.

On a yearly basis, I used to visit my grandmother's senior center. One of the center's common problems was that the seniors needed to go to the washroom frequently. Some of them needed to go every five to 10 minutes, and they needed assistance to complete their business. However, when the seniors were in the game room playing cards, they could stay for the whole afternoon without going to the washroom. They became involved in the games.

The examples above show that people need to get involved in a social and interactive process in order to stay focused.

When students stay inside the classroom to study, the study becomes the subject matter. When students get "into" an activity, they become socially interactive and collaborate with others to complete their schoolwork. In this case, the students become the subject matter, and the study becomes secondary and subservient. Students want to get involved in an activity and become the subject matter.

In *The Child and the Curriculum*, the classic education book referred to earlier, the author, Dewey, wrote, "The child is the starting point, the center, and the end. His development, his growth, is the ideal." In other words, study is subservient. "It is he, and not the subject-matter which determines both quality and quantity of learning," Dewey further wrote. So readers, we need to position students in the main role, and ask them to take charge of their study.

Students can recognize tangible things more easily. Visible things are memorable. They mostly imagine the things that they see, hear, feel, touch, and smell. So it is hard for students to separate activity from work. Therefore, we have to combine activity and work in order for students to stimulate their interests in their subject courses.

Activity originates from real work, such as real planting, cultivating, inventing with materials, and the physical activity involved. The activity doesn't involve real material but uses symbolic and representative objectives to act as the work. For example, students may use chairs to represent locomotives and brooms to represent horses or airplanes. In game play, students drive the cars, do banking, buy real estate and invest stocks, but these items are all symbolic, not real.

Therefore, activity is highly educative to the imagination and for spiritual appreciation. When students are playing and involved in activities, they are free. They don't think too much about the expected results, but engage in a joyous, spiritual, and imaginative process. Therefore, their activities become educative and appreciated.

Study is the activity that follows a professor's instructions, according to school curriculums. Study needs to fulfill a certain task, either to complete homework or to finish certain experiments. It needs real physical involvement. It is results-driven and utilitarian. Most of the time, study is filled with difficulties and unknowns. With dislike and with great patience, students complete their homework to meet the requirements of courses and to earn credits. Students study passively because they have to, not because they want to. Students are expecting results and hope that study will end soon. When they have completed their homework, most of them say, "Finally."

Most of the time, however, students are not anticipating the end of an activity when it is fun and inspirational. In fact, they wish that it could go on longer. Furthermore, the activity often inspires them to think outside the box and come up with creative solutions. For example, Harry Potter rode his broom and flew to the sky, overcoming his temporary difficulties. An inspirational activity can lead to new ways of solving problems.

Since activity creates a fun learning environment, why don't more people implement active learning? Simply put, many students are just focused on earning high marks because they know that this is what college admissions officers are looking for. Grades are easier to measure than soft qualities like musicality, athleticism, morality, and social skills. Some universities strictly state that they only accept students who have grade averages of more than 90 percent. So it is not hard to understand why many high school students just aim for high marks. They focus only on their course material, because they believe mixing activity with study will drag their grades down.

The truth is we were born for happiness, fun, and play, so it is hard for many students to separate studying from having fun.

Many parents become angry when they see their children playing while studying. Traditionally, parents expect their children to sit up straight at their desk, solely focused on their textbooks and course materials. The parents believe that this is the correct way to study and tell their children that playtime and study don't mix. In fact, some parents discipline their children when they catch them playing while doing homework, because to them, playing has no academic benefit.

Of course, the opposite is true. Study with an attitude of play embeds interest in objective form through the use of course material. Converting study into free play inspires development.

As students, how do you convert your study into activities involving learning?

Instead of sitting at a desk and reading your textbook, consider self- or group activities. Converting study into activity embeds the course material into the activity.

1. Take a piece of blank paper, give yourself one or two minutes, and then write about the lesson that you have studied. You may also give a real-life example for the same topic. Clarify the muddiest point in your study. Be specific (self-activity).

2. Write a daily journal about what you have learned. How do you interpret the course material? How do you apply the course material to the real world (self-activity)?

3. In the middle of class, write about your feelings about class, the teacher, and what you're taking away from the teacher's presentation. For example, "I am so surprised that . . . (the fact). I have learned that . . . (take away). I wonder what . . . (questions to ask)." This could summarize your response to the teacher's demonstration. When the class is dismissed, you then could ask questions regarding what was unclear. This self Q & A

session will stimulate your critical thinking and illuminate the ideas presented by the teacher (self-activity).

4. Prepare for class by roughly browsing the textbook for what you are going to learn the next day. You will discover what you have understood and identify what is important to you (self-activity).

5. Create a group discussion. Form a group of students, give each person an index card, and ask them to write one concern about the course material. All the students then can deposit their card into a fish bowl. Then have one of them draw a card from the fish bowl and ask what the students are thinking regarding the concern before reading out the card. This encourages students to explore major themes, compare views and applications, and foster their higher-order thinking skills. This method greatly increases their engagement and learning effectiveness. You could design your group discussion in a more creative and fun way. For example, you could use hand signs to express whether you agree with the idea; you also could use flash cards; sometimes, you could even prepare a small gift for the winner (group activity).

6. Sometimes, you could have a few good friends get together and ask that each one come up with a quotation in relation to the points you learned in the course. You could use a quotation from a famous person. If you could not find one in your research, you could come up with one on your own. But most importantly, you need to find out the relationship between the positions that each person advocates and what you have taken away from the course. This exercise develops critical thinking and analysis skills (group activity).

7. A survey done by one university found that students learned more from their roommates than their professor or the classmates they met inside the classroom. A dormitory is a family model.

There, the students openly guide and help one another. This is the place where students are encouraged to cooperate, rather than compete. If one roommate is sick or does not have good note-taking skills, he could get help from other roommates and fill in the gaps in his notes. Sometimes, they could form a dorm forum for a specific topic. They could state their own views, hear from others, and hone their argumentative skills. Each roommate would hold themselves accountable to the others. Therefore, no one should get lazy (group activity).

8. Make your best friend your accountability partner. A friend is like a mirror. Your best friend understands you the most. He/she can tell you what is right or what is wrong by looking at your face. From your conversation, the friend can find out what had made you happy, what had discouraged you, or what triumphs or challenges that you have had. Ask your best friend whether he/she could be your accountability partner. He must be fully open to you. He must be willing to help you or criticize you, if needed. Most importantly, he/she must be able to evaluate your work, give critical feedback, carry necessary and constructive arguments, and help correct mistakes in problem solving. You, as the receiver, are also required to be fully open to receive the comments. Never feel embarrassed if the feedback is negative. Receiving negative feedback does not mean that you have failed, but that you are growing, even though you don't feel comfortable.

There is some light difference between friends and partners. Between friends, you are willing to do things without expecting anything in return. Sometimes, you could also compromise a friend's mistake by keeping silent. But as accountability partners, you need to speak up whenever it is needed. You scratch his back, and he scratches yours.

Sometimes, the scratching can be painful. But you still have to scratch (group activity).

1. For some research programs, it is hard to complete the whole project. Instead, you pitch your ideas to different students and ask them if they are interested in joining you for the project. Each student in the group is asked to complete some distinct part of it. Once the students have completed their work, they can join it together to finish the entire project. For example, if the students want to find out a way to improve the tap water quality in the city of Toronto, they can form a group of students for that purpose. One student may be good at chemical experiments and would be responsible for that part of the work. Another student, skilled in communication, could go to city hall to find out what support that they could receive from the city. Each student could demonstrate their different part of the project, then conduct regular meetings to put the project together and get feedback to improve their strategy for their portion (group activity).

2. Acting out what you have learned through drama and role-play gives you a deeper, better, and more pleasant recollection of the knowledge. In a created drama, you could also add your new ideas and way of looking at things. You could debate what you have learned from the course and how you want to reflect and apply what you have learned in the modern world. For example, in a French class, students were asked to create a show that reflected a historical character in France. Two students chose Eugène-René Poubelle, who invented the garbage can. The students presented the storyline—why and how Poubelle invented the garbage can. Many people threw their garbage into the street from the window. It was a horrible thing. To protect

the environment, Poubelle created a garbage can to collect the waste. From this presentation, students learned the French language, the history, about the invention and environmental protection, and moreover, they fostered a deep love of learning. This activity directed the future interest of one of the course's students, a young man who had attended Canada's St. Andrew's College and went on to enroll in America's Columbia University. Below is his short journal entry.

In grade 3, I fell in love with the French culture. It was not only the natural flow of the language that I admired, but also the culture.

"Bonjour, c'est moi," I said as I knocked on the door. I was acting in a school video project and I was Eugène-René Poubelle, the person who introduced the garbage can in Paris. I became engrossed in my role, dressing up in a white shirt, grey cardigan and the iconic French moustache. As I took a look at myself in the mirror, I reflected on the meaning behind the moustache that I wore.

It was not just a moustache; it was a piece of art. The tips were elegantly curled, showing the culture's grace and refined taste. The time it took to fashion the moustache into its shape is indicative of the emphasis French people place on having a polished image. More importantly the moustache is made out of love and creativity, core values of French culture. As I wore that moustache, I strived to show the essence of French culture.

Laughter and applause came from the audience as they indulged in my interpretation of

Eugène-René Poubelle. But more importantly, it reminded me of why I loved French culture: its elegance, creativity, and love.

Columbia's Maison Française provides an atmosphere for French education that cannot be matched. I plan to spend time in the Maison Française through the Café Conversation sessions on the 2nd floor of Buell Hall, the Book Club discussions on works such as No et Moi and the weekly gatherings to appreciate French culture. Having been in the rigorous extended French program at St. Andrew's College, I wish to continue French study by taking courses such as FREN W3333.

I earnestly hope to don the Columbia blue next year as I pursue a double major in French in conjunction with business management.

1. By creating an online forum to use social media for discussion and debate, you can meet students who are focused on the same project worldwide. You are absorbing a diversified, worldwide opinion in your niche through debate. Upon receiving others' comments on your ideas, you know what to improve next. Social media is a convenient way to spread your message more widely and quickly. In the physical world, you meet limited numbers of people in one day; but in the virtual world, you meet thousands of readers in a few seconds. You will be surprised at how many comments you will receive in such a short time. Furthermore, it is more fun to read online with images, video, and sound. There is no comparison. But you need to take time to establish your social platform. Read different articles every day, give comments, like others' ideas, or share your own. Day by day, you will create your social platform. Once you have some ideas, you will receive an instant response (self- and group activity). The

platform will provide you huge support for brainstorming your project.

2. Playing physical games or computer games is a nuisance to many parents and schoolteachers, because the students involved in the games have trouble stopping. Therefore, they may leave homework or a project unfinished. Playing games can distract students and affect their study negatively. But it is undeniable that many games combine education with play. The designer of the games may have created them for an educational purpose by including the scientific method or the laws of nature; but if the students misuse it, then it may cause bad results.

As long as you can control the amount of playing time, games are a good way to introduce the scientific concept and test hypotheses as the game proceeds. They deliver the concepts in a fun way rather than a theoretical way. Playing games and apps on a phone helps students develop their intellectual capacity. For some talented students, they could create apps according to their interests.

Activity-based learning builds up the students' personality and character. Through activity-based learning, students develop their interpersonal and intrapersonal skills by interactive activities. Through self-activity, the student gains a deeper understanding of himself/ herself. By role-play within group activity, students learn to collaborate and cooperate with other students. It is a big part of learning and growing. Activity-based learning gives students a great opportunity to learn, grow, and gain trust by asking them to take responsibility for themselves. Through activity-based learning, students actually manage themselves. So there is no discipline problem. It boosts the students' confidence, self-esteem, independence, and self-management skills. Activity-based learning also allows students to learn at their own speed, without being taunted by classmates or scolded by teachers.

Activity-based learning provides a pleasant and relaxed environment, dividing the organic physical and psychological distance between students and their peers and between teachers and students. These activities encourage personal growth through students' involvement, fostering their eagerness and thirst for knowledge, and reinforcing their development of competence. Lastly, and most importantly, the activity stretches their scope of creativity.

The students' personality and character have more value than the subject matter; they are the real business of the study. To that end, the purpose of the study is not about marks on a report card. It is not the knowledge and information that students have mastered; it is about self-realization, self-growth, and self-development. That is the goal of study. Like Dewey wrote in *The Child and the Curriculum*, "To possess all the world of knowledge and lose one's own self is as awful a fate in education as in religion."

There is a conflict for students between their natural beliefs and the practical needs of their study life. Naturally, every student wants to have fun; but, practically, they cannot get into the university they want if they don't have good marks. How do we solve this problem?

SELF-GROWTH.
SELF-DEVELOPMENT
& FUN LEARNING   MARKS

First of all, students need to consider this question: Do you really believe that you can secure a good job in the future without soft-quality education? I highly doubt it. Many university graduates cannot find a job for a long time after graduating because they lack the soft qualities that employers seek. Nowadays, employers care more about their employees' attitudes. They don't really care about the academic marks as long as they are within an acceptable range. What matters to them are the extracurricular activities the students engaged in outside the classroom. Every student does the same thing inside the classroom, but their attitude and what they do outside the classroom make them stand out. The employers see the young graduates as pieces of blank paper; they are fresh, naïve, and filled with dreams. If they choose to work with the graduates who have good attitudes, then they can teach them about anything and everything. From there, the graduates can learn and grow. So we must stop thinking that activity-based learning is not important. In this type of learning, students have opportunities to cooperate with others. The collaboration fosters students' ability to be well rounded. As such, the traditional learning method, putting the students in oceans of Q & As for the refinement of the marks, is unnecessary.

Second, the way for students to have fun and get A's is to combine study with activity. This method of learning satisfies the students' emotional happiness, utilizes their playful minds, and meets the real needs of learning. It is easy, fast, and, most importantly, a fun way to learn.

For example, St. Andrew's College promotes the methodology of activity-based learning. Most of the parents understand the slogan "Boys should grow up in the field, not inside the classroom" by its founder Rev. Dr. George Bruce. But they do not always understand the idea of the "complete man and well-rounded citizen." I am one of them. I even asked the assistant headmaster, Michael Paluch, "What does that mean?" As the boys grow a few inches taller, the parents start to realize that they not only are committed academically, but also are taking full charge in athletics, music, or the arts. St. Andrew's also widely fosters students' social interests and social contributions through outreach programs and innovative adventures. Each year, the students share their business ventures (problem-based learning, solutions to real-life problems) with business programs with the local community (www.sac.on.ca/news/detail.aspx?LinkId=3758&ModuleId=193). Activity-based learning allows students to visit a European museum in history class, travel to the mountains for geography, and explore the world (www.sac.on.ca/upper-school/explore-the-world/index.aspx). The experiences that they gain outside the classroom imprint comprehensive knowledge of critical thinking, politics, and geography. Some days may be rewarding, some days may be exhausting. But the students develop their own interests during the journey. Most importantly, they learn to work with their classmates and create a lifetime brotherhood bond. St. Andrew's College provides continuous opportunities to foster the students' intellectual capacity, social adaptability, and spiritual richness through music, athletic clubs, debate, community service, group projects, the element of competition, theater, visual arts, and chapel. The students start their day with prayer. They use real-life activities to reflect and create mirror images of the content from the classroom.

Third, we ask students to take action, not solely focusing on the subject matter, but also by making learning a social and interactive process. We also ask students to understand fully that part of study is to share the social consciousness as well as adjust the individual activity. Students will thrive when they experience and interact with the curriculum.

Activity-based learning allows students to break their study content into different small increments, master them at a self-selected pace, and complete the entire material serially. It makes the students less teacher-dependent. When their study is activity-based, they will be more interested in a course and will get the idea more quickly. Therefore, they don't feel that they are studying; they are not expecting results, but enjoying the journey and sticking to it, never anticipating the end. Study, like play, helps students stay focused and inspires their self-realization. They manifest likeable results.

If students purely focus on subject matter and marks, study becomes work. Because of the utilitarian nature of the approach, study becomes mechanical and dead. Activity-based learning—converting study into play—grounds play into study, and makes study more fun, positive, and constructive. Activity-based learning makes study more vital and active. It builds up the imaginary world alongside the tangibility of actual study. Activity-based learning enlarges the students' thinking.

Activity-based learning is a tool to foster imagination. For example, it is how a child finds the meaning of a broom by first thinking of it as a horse or the meaning of other things by applying creative thinking. Through activity and play, students discover the identities and meanings for their real learning. Activity-based learning is a big part of intellectual development and personal growth.

Activity forms past efforts and experiences into future endeavors for a student. Learning is active. It involves reaching beyond the mind. Activity-based learning is the organic assimilation starting from within. The students' growth  and development doesn't mean just getting things out of their minds, but it is the development of one experience into a more desired experience.

Solely focusing on the study material and educative medium makes it impossible to enrich the powers and interest within students, which is valuable to function. The educative medium of the course materials must be maneuvered, and the manner in which they maneuver around them will depend almost entirely upon the stimuli. Activities are the best way to stimulate the students' knowledge of their materials.

John Zhang was a university teacher who taught electrical engineering. In his Power Supply course, the students were sleepy and bored when he taught theory. They did not seem to care about the details of ground connection, short circuit, and over-currency protection.

One day Professor Zhang decided to introduce some activities. He asked five students to come to the stage and perform what happened underground in regard to ground connection, short circuit, and over-current protection for underground mining.

He cited the following case:

About 4,000 feet underground, the mice were very hungry. There were rocks, coal, metals, and minerals. There was no food underground. The mice found many big, fat cable pipelines lying down there. So the mice were very interested in and curious about the pipelines. So they went to have a bite. The mice bit a cable line, the rubber was gone and so were all the metal lines connected to one point. These lines were not supposed to connect to each other, but it happened. Suddenly the whole electrical circuit short-circuited. There was lightning, smoke, and all the lines were burned. Fortunately, before the problem got bigger, the over- currency protector engaged. The switch on the break was off, so the whole circuit, people, and equipment underground were protected. However, they had to stay in the dark for a while until the maintenance people arrived to fix the whole problem.

After students acted out the incident Professor Zhang described, they and their classmates looked forward to attending each of his classes, hoping they or their peers would be asked to re-enact another accident. Waiting for accidents? What a class! When the problem occurred, the students could understand why what they learned was so meaningful.

Lack of activity, lack of motivation, and lack of play make learning mechanical and lifeless. When material is directly supplied in the form of a lesson to be learned as a lesson, the textbook is the only source of knowledge. The teacher takes more responsibility, and the connecting links of need and aim are conspicuous for their

absence. Once students lack motivation, study becomes aimless or utilitarian, automated and cold.

Learning must be organic and vital. It must be equated with interaction and activity. Activity-based learning is the play of mental demand and material supply. If educators would recognize this, then students would be happier and social waste would be reduced (organic environmental protection in modern study).

To make the learning process more active, so students can understand more, apply more, and achieve more, we need to understand that achieving high marks should not be the only goal. Studying inside the classroom, focusing solely on the subject matter, can be a waste.

Chapter 4

Study Less and Achieve More

Today, society is busy and complicated. School is the same way. Many times, the school, the teachers, and society need students to complete a large amount of homework assignments. Students need to complete these assignments in a timely and productive manner in order to meet the curriculum standards.

All these expectations and society's needs stresses students. They are overwhelmed by too many demanding assignments, not to mention the high number of standardized tests that are placed on their shoulders. This does not even factor in that the standards of learning are increased annually.

What do you do when you have too many assignments? Avoid them? Not a good idea. So then, what *do* you do? Very simple: You face the work, but you must also create a solution for handling it. If you don't release yourself from the stress, you will get low grades and will be left behind.

To solve your problem, you need to identify it first. Assess how many assignments you have. Daily, keep track of them in a notebook. Browse the list and prioritize your assignments—determine what you will do and in what order. Create a daily and weekly To-Do List.

Your To-Do List should be realistic, based on the length of time it typically takes you to complete tasks. If you're scheduled to complete a large project in a very short time, you're likely already intimidated by the assignment and you begin to struggle as you approach it. You want to quit before you've even begun. Not good. But that said, your goal cannot be too small either. If it is, it does not serve the need. Now, for each task, commit to a specific time frame that allots for work and fun. That means in addition to work, you need to schedule break time, eating time, and time for playing games.

You must have a clear mind. A clear mind always says "yes," but a confused mind always says "no." A clear mind also includes that you declare your goal to everybody, such as your parents, your relatives, your family members, your roommates, your friends, your classmates—anybody who is near you. For example, you tell them, "My name is Jessica, and I am going to do math homework, chapter two, from page 29 to 35 from seven p.m. to eight p.m. Please don't disturb me." When you begin your homework, shut off your cell phone and ignore your social media accounts. Stay off the Internet unless it is for research purposes related to your assignment. Don't veer from your academic task.

Every night, check your progress and readjust your plan and schedule.

Think positively! Every half hour, go over what you have done and declare your victory, such as, "My name is Jessica, and I have completed page 29 to 31 from seven p.m. to seven thirty p.m. I feel great, and I am very proud of myself." You may take a sip of juice and tell yourself that you deserve it. Recognize that you have done half of the math already! It is almost finished! Be good and keep going!

To study efficiently, you also need to position yourself properly.

Create your own feng shui for your place of study. What is feng shui? It means "wind-water" and is one of the "Five Arts of Chinese Metaphysics," according to Wikipedia. In this art, Wikipedia says, architecture is "discussed" as a force ("qi") that binds "the universe, earth, and humanity."

How can we interpret feng shui in modern culture? Feng shui is when you place certain furniture in certain positions; it creates proper walking and working flow. This creates enough space for people to feel comfortable and to be filled with harmony. This means good feng shui. Good feng shui gives people a good feeling and smoothes out their energy and joy. With these feelings, people can fulfill certain tasks quickly and efficiently. Once you place yourself in an environment with good feng shui, you will say to yourself, "I want to do this. I can do this. I will do this fast. No problem."

For example, the bedroom or bed does not provide good feng shui for studying. When you stay in the bedroom, the first thing you think about is sleep and you relax. You become drowsy, you want to lie down, and you don't have the spirit for working hard any longer. Another example, the kitchen does not have good feng shui for studying either. When you are in the kitchen, the first thing you are thinking about is eating a good, tasty meal. When you are in front of a fruit basket or in front of a dining table full of delicious dishes, you will be guaranteed that you want to start the meal by stopping your mouth from watering as soon as possible. Another example is the couch, which does not have good feng shui for studying. The couch is a place for us to take a break, take a nap, or watch TV. Once you place yourself on the couch, you feel restful. If you are very tired, you could fall to sleep within five minutes.

Having said that, where can you find good feng shui for studying? There are many places, including a library, classroom, office room in your house, and so on. How can you create your own feng shui for studying?

- Have a solid chair to support your body and your back. With that solid chair, you can wave your legs freely when you get tired.
- Have a bright light so that you don't need to look hard at your computer and books.
- Maintain a certain level of quiet. It is hard to stay focused in a noisy environment.
- Study in a place that has fresh airflow and a good temperature. Keep proper airflow in the study room by opening the window for a short while. The temperature should not be overly warm, but a bit cool, not cold. The environment should keep you alert.
- Study in a place that is big enough for you to stand up and make your positive declaration mentioned previously. If you have many people around you, you still need to stand up; just don't shout! Say quietly to yourself, "My name is Jessica, and I will complete my math homework from seven p.m. to eight p.m. today, September 30th. And I am a good girl!" or when you complete it, stand up and say, "Yeah!"
- Always bring treats to your study sessions. During your break, reward yourself with them and say aloud, "Life is so good, life is great."

To summarize the above, a good feng shui place for studying is a place that makes you feel excited, interested, and makes you want to start studying right away. From there you become unstoppable until you finish what you are doing.

Studying is like dancing. You need to follow a certain rhythm. What is the rhythm? The rhythm is the time frame in which you intend to complete your work. You keep to your plan; do it, do it, do it like the waltz—dong-cha-cha, dong-cha-cha.

If you don't plan to finish your work by a specific deadline, the chances are that it will take you forever to complete it. Don't be the person who operates like that.

Here's an idea: Start your work every forty-five minutes, stop ten minutes for a break, and then start again. When you have completed one homework assignment, place a sticky star on the edge of your paper or draw a smiley face, then start your next assignment.

You need to stay on pace until you have completed all your scheduled day's assignments. Sometimes, no matter what you do, a project can take more time than you had planned. When that happens, don't beat yourself over the head, just extend your time automatically, but not for too long. The next day, readjust your plan so that you can keep your rhythm and keep your confidence for your dancing (ahem, I mean studying).

Here is the question: What if you are just too tired to catch up on all your homework?

The answer is simple: Take a nap! Exhaustion will not help you learn. Be honest with yourself and satisfy your body's need for rest as soon as possible.

Don Hahn, the producer of *The Lion King* and *Beauty and Beast*, suggested that every company mandate employees nap in the middle of the workday. His idea is a good one.

A small nap, especially in the middle of the workday, is mysterious and enjoyable. In just a few minutes, you can fall into a deep dream. Not long afterward, you wake up feeling wonderful. Your entire body is rested well; you feel as fresh as a baby. After your nap, you give 100 percent of yourself and full attention to what you are doing. You become efficient.

Many successful people nap to stay energetic. Premier Zhou EnLai, a prime minister of China, worked an average of eighteen hours a day. He often napped while sitting in a car or on breaks between meetings. For him, a ten-minute nap was like one hour's worth of sleep. He was recognized as one of the world leaders who slept the least. Another famous napper is the mayor of the city of Mississauga in Ontario, Hazel McCallion. Take a lesson from this story: McCallion was more than eighty-five years old when she visited China. During a special music performance on one of her many stops, she joined the show, singing songs like the performers. Between music sets, she took a very short nap. When it was her turn to get up and sing again, a nearby audience member called on her. She woke up. "Oh, it's my turn?" she asked. Then she started singing again.

The moral of the story: Taking a small nap can put you on the road to more efficient studying. Without a nap, your body is half-awake, half-asleep. You will spend more time studying but complete less work.

Is there any magic way to arrange our time so that we have enough of it to complete our homework and projects, participate in sports, watch music shows, and pursue personal hobbies?

Big rocks first

The number-one thing is that you have to manage your time and priorities. If you have several projects or homework assignments at the same time, make sure that you take care of the important ones first. These assignments are your "big rocks."

Stephen R. Covey is one of the greatest authors in the world. In his book *First Things First*, he describes a lecture in which the presenter placed a wide-mouth jar on a table beside some fist-sized rocks, then proceeded to fill the jar to the brim with the rocks. The presenter asked the audience if the jar was full and received a round reply of "Yes!" Well, the audience was . . . wrong! According to Covey, the presenter then put more items into the jar—gravel, a bucketful of sand, even a pitcher of water—to make the larger point that "if you don't put the big rocks in first . . . would you ever have gotten any of them in?"

This little story can be applied to all aspects of your study, planning, and time management. For example, think of its application in the following scenario: Let's say you have to design a marketing plan for a company, complete a math assignment, study for a macroeconomics exam, and hold homecoming for new students—and you need to perform all these tasks around the same time.

The question then becomes, out of all these activities, which ones are the big rocks? More importantly, are you making sure that you are putting the big rocks into the jar first?

Remember, the big rocks are the most important and urgent thing.

When you put in your effort to "complete" your big rocks, you always have time and space to fit your small rocks, your sand, and your water into your jar. But, if you put in your small rocks first, your sand, your water, and the big rocks will never fit. So what's the story's moral? If you pay attention to the small things first, you will never have the time and energy to complete the important things.

What are your big rocks? Please take time to figure it out.

Nancy registered for Robert G. Allen's Fortune in You course. In the course, she found her big purpose for her life. She found out that she was born to be a great real estate investor and to help many other investors. Her daily ritual is:

- Walking from eight a.m. to nine a.m. (as her health comes first). While she is taking the walk, she is meditating on her goal of reaching two hundred units in the next five years.
- Advertising to get more investors. Her goal is to have three hundred names in her database each month. She's already found about thirty serious investors. Out of those investors, three are desperately looking to purchase rental properties and generate passive income.
- After seven p.m., she makes herself available to help her son with his writing assignments. She considers her son her big rock too.
- She connects with her team members every day, meets them twice a week, and has telephone conferences the rest of the days.
- She meets two investors daily.
- She spends adequate time relaxing and having fun in between her important tasks.

These first five things are her big rocks, and they are non-negotiable.

Stick to your plan

It is very easy for people to make plans, but not so easy to execute them. That is why fitness centers have more members in January than the other months—most of us have New Years' resolutions that we just aren't able to keep! To stay on schedule, you need to follow an exercise for acting out your plan mentally and physically. After that, you will enter a condition of following your plan automatically. Sticking to your plan until the very end will become second nature.

First, determine why you have put your current plan in place. The exercise should help reinforce your faith and desire to stick to your plan on a daily basis for at least twenty-one consecutive days.

Declare your goal. In T. Harv Eker's "90 Day Wealth Conditioning Program," Eker recommends using "VAKS" (Visual, Auditory, Kinesthetic, and Spirit) for making a declaration. For our purposes, students can use VAKS to make a declaration that will help them stay on schedule.

1.   **Visual.** Clasp your hands with your thumbs pointing up, and move your arms to the left, creating a figure "8" while moving your eyes but not your head. This exercise helps the left brain and right brain work together.

2.   **Auditory.** From the top and down the outer rim, repeatedly massage your ears for thirty seconds as you make your declaration.

3.   **Kinesthetic.** While standing, bend your right arm and raise it, then lift your knee and twist yourself so that your elbow and knee touch. Then do the same thing with your left arm and right knee. For thirty seconds, take turns repeating the exercise on both sides of your body as you make your declaration.

4.   **Spirit.** With your hands on top of your heart and your eyes closed, say your declaration out loud for thirty seconds and feel your voice vibrate.

The twenty-one-day exercise could be:
Day one: July 1, 2014

1.   Declare the purpose of your goal by using VAKS.
2.   Clarify your intention (why).
3.   Acknowledge five successful things that you have enjoyed today.

Day two: July 2, 2014

1. Set your attitude for your goal declarations by using VAKS.
2. Describe how you will add value to others' lives once you reach your goal.
3. Acknowledge your three successful stories and describe how you enjoyed them.

Day three: July 3, 2014

1. Declare your goal by using VAKS.
2. Describe why you believe that you have the ability to complete your goal and why you deserve to be successful in doing so.
3. Acknowledge your successes.

Day four: July 4, 2014

1. Declare your goal by using VAKS.
2. Describe your daily challenges. Further describe the actions you have taken to move yourself forward through the challenges. Write down the steps that you took in spite of fear and negative feelings. Describe how you overcame the challenges and how you felt that you were growing.
3. Acknowledge your successes.

Day five: July 5, 2014

1. Declare your goals with VAKS.
2. Describe one thing/person you are grateful for. Further describe how the thing/person helps you and why you are grateful for this. Write down how it makes you feel.
3. Acknowledge your successes.

The above is only a five-day example. You can create your own for additional days. The purpose of this exercise is to reinforce your goal and to determine why you want to achieve it. What would happen if your goal became a reality? How would you feel? VAKS helps you discover your subconscious mind and reasoning and to envision yourself in the future. Every time you state your goals aloud—"auditory"—you are telling your mind what you want to complete. This increases your faith and makes you believe in yourself. That said, kinesthetic movement engenders a burning desire to achieve your goal. You need to make it happen right away. And through spirit affirmation, you put your faith not only in your mind, but also in your heart. Your faith becomes second nature.

Principle and application

When you do your homework, pay attention to the principle first, not questions.

It does not matter which course you are studying or which chapter you are studying. There is a principle, such as in physics, F=ma is one of Newton's Laws of Motion, where "F" is the net force acting on the object, "m" is the mass of the object, and "a" is the acceleration of the object. The equation describes the relationship between a body and the forces acting upon it and its motion in response to said forces. It can be summarized as follows:

First Law: When viewed in an inertial reference frame, an object either is at rest or moves at a constant velocity, unless acted upon by an external force.

Second Law: The acceleration of a body is directly proportional to, and in the same direction as, the net force acting on the body, and inversely proportional to its mass.

Third Law: When one body exerts a force on a second body, the second body simultaneously exerts a force equal in magnitude and opposite in direction to that of the first body.

To make things simple, you only need to understand this formula. Then you automatically know how to implement this theory to many different questions and answers.

However, if you don't review the principle, and instead jump into questions right away, you will find yourself drowning in an ocean of questions. This idea applies to many types of studies. By the same token, millions of questions can be asked in different ways. If you understand the principle, all the questions become very simple.

Here is the question, "Are you going to study the questions (millions) or are you going to study the principle (one)?" Once you understand the principle, even the questions are asked in many different ways and you can answer them all by using the principle freely.

Without understanding the principle, you jump into the questions right away. Could you study them all? Do you have time to study them all? The answer is obvious—"NO."

Danger! If you immerse yourself in an ocean of questions, you will become exhausted and eventually drown.

Eighty percent of the time, study the principle, and 20 percent of the time, study the questions and answers.

Group activity

Student Jack has an apple, and he sits alone. He can only eat his apple. Student John has an orange and sits by himself. He can only eat his orange. But think about this: If they cut their fruits and place them on a plate, then sit together, they can eat both the apple and orange. What if we have three students with three kinds of fruits, four students with four kinds of fruits, five students with five kinds of fruits, etcetera? If we cut all kinds of fruits and all the students sit together, all of the students can eat all of the fruits. Do you think that these students feel happier? The answer is yes.

Nowadays, many schools don't allow their students to copy their homework from each other, but the schools allow their students to help each other. You study together and do the work together. By the end, you use your own words and sentences to write your ideas and solutions for the project.

There is a Chinese saying: "san ge chou pi jian, sheng guo yi ge zhu ge lian." In Chinese it is written: "三个臭皮匠胜过一个诸葛亮。" This means three dumb people together are better than one genius. Each person is an individual; each person has his/her own personality and wisdom. By working together, people share ideas with each other, helping each other. Each of you is benefiting from other people's talent. Each of you is leveraging other people's wisdom. So together, three people are better than one.

In school, there is competition. Some students don't want to share their ideas with other people. They think that if they tell their ideas to other people, other people may become better than them.

Don't underestimate other people's intelligence. Even though they may be weak in some areas, they may be strong in others. By helping other people, they stay in gratitude and want to help you in return. They appreciate you so much that they will do anything for you voluntarily.

The worst words in the world would be, "I know it" or "I am a great person, and I don't need other people's help." The moment that you are thinking about that, you are full of yourself. You don't have any room for other people to help you; therefore, you don't have room to grow. You will forever stay at the level you are at now. Do you think that you will stay there? Are you sure that you will be at the same level forever? Here is the bad news for you: If you are not growing, you are dying. There is no way that you can stay at the same level. There is no in-between. You are growing or you are dying. There is no "staying" in the world.

Grace's son, Liche, ranked number three in the physics competition nationwide, and while in high school, he was recruited to Beijing University. Now, every day his university classmates ask him many questions about math, physics, and chemistry. He answers each question patiently. Of course, he loses much of his time by doing this. What does he gain? He gains much by helping other people. He becomes stronger than before, because teaching other people how to study is one of the best ways to learn. Because he repeats the same thing many times, his skills and knowledge in those areas becomes second nature. He can use them freely when he needs to. In those specific areas, he becomes stronger and stronger.

Have you ever found that you are more energetic when you are in a group? Have you ever found that you are happier when you are in a group? Have you ever found that it is more fun when you are in a group? I bet that you have.

Have you ever had a problem when your parents ask you to play the piano or other instruments? Have you ever had an argument when you are assigned a schedule for practicing the piano? Have you ever felt that it is boring to play piano? Have you ever thought to quit the piano and sell that sucker to someone else?

We already know the answer: You have. You want to stop playing the piano and sell it because it bores you. You hate practicing.

Have you ever felt bored playing in the school band? Most of you will say no. Why? Because when you are in a group, playing in a band with your peers is fun. What bores you is playing solo (like practicing piano at home).

What do you learn by playing with other people in a band? You learn to play the note right, otherwise your voice in a band becomes a noise. You also have to learn to play that right note in the right time, including the length of each note and starting point of each note. What if you play the right note at the wrong time? Then you play the wrong note.

What do you learn from the band? You learn to cooperate with others by watching your team members and to keep the same pace. You learn how to do teamwork. You learn more by playing in a band than you do playing solo.

What if you forget the note or you do not play your part? Don't worry too much. You have support from your team; therefore, you do not leave a "blank" (silent) moment for your audience.

You feel so great now. The world is changing. To learn to work with a team is an important ingredient for your future success.

Study buddy

Have you ever made a buddy (your sister or your brother) in your school? Have you ever made good friends so that they will help you voluntarily whenever you need? If you have not, you better make at least one.

> *"Coming together is a beginning; keeping together*
> *is progress; working together is success."*
> **—Henry Ford**

When people are working together, they become more energetic and are inspired by other people.

Accountability partner

Do you have an accountability partner? You ask, what is that?

Example: Kathy has been out of shape for many years. Every year, her resolution for the New Year is to lose weight. Her plan is:

- Walk an hour each day for the first month, and run forty minutes starting the second month. Continue running for forty minutes for the rest of the year.
- Eat healthy food. Eat seven servings of vegetables per day. Eat white meat only.
- Take vitamin and mineral supplements every day.

Kathy started her plan on the first day of the year. She felt very good on the first day because her steps were not heavy anymore, and her heart beat fast. Her whole body was filled with energy.

On the third day, an emergency arose, and she could not walk. She said that was okay because she had already exercised for two days.

On the fourth day, a snowstorm blew in, making it unsafe to go outdoors. Kathy stayed home.

On the fifth day, the weather was fine, Kathy's schedule was open, but she felt lazy. She did not want to go anymore. She had given up.

In February, intense stomach pain landed Kathy in a hospital emergency room. With each small step she took, she felt dreadful pain. She was diagnosed with liver fat filtration. The doctor asked her many questions and concluded that the liver fat filtration was due to obesity.

Kathy was on the verge of liver failure. The liver is the biggest and the most important organ inside the body. Without a working liver, Kathy's life was in danger. Therefore, she decided that she would lose thirty pounds no matter what.

How? She contacted her friend Kim, who also needed to lose weight. Kim became her accountability partner. They made a plan. Their plans were:

- To write down what they had eaten each day, including big meals, snacks, vegetables, and fruits, and to record the beverages they drank. They also had to write down the time they consumed their meals and the amount they ate.

- To meet every week to check each other's notebook.
- To act as if they were world-class nutrition experts and give advice to each other on their eating habits, and how to improve their eating habits.
- To walk to the coffee shop between both of their houses, say good morning, and walk back to their homes.
- To keep walking on snowy days, but go to the gym on rainy days.
- To voluntarily help the other person.
- To be tough. They would both act like disciplinarians and drive the other person to achieve her goals.
- To use a special scale and ruler to check body mass, body weight, body fat, and waist size every week.

The two friends were very passionate about their plans, schedule, and actions. However, they were intimidated, especially by the idea of acting like world-class nutrition experts, which they knew they were not. Nevertheless, in order to give other people advice, you need to be an expert. How? Thanks to computers: the Internet, Google, and other sources, such as Wikipedia, online doctors, weight-loss forums, eHow, etc. These resources make research very easy. Kathy did thirty minutes of research every day. Some of the research results were fun, including topics such as:

- Food ingredients
- How to cook tasty and healthy meals
- Think you have lost weight?
- Is your figure good?

- Think that you are healthy? Lose weight and become healthy in your mind first, your body second.

Three months after Kathy and Kim began working out together, Kathy lost twenty pounds and Kim lost thirty-five.

Kim is a go-getter and was very tough on Kathy. Kathy got mad sometimes, but she was happy when she saw her results. She went to the hospital for a follow-up appointment and found out that the liver fat filtration had reversed itself. She was healthy again. From the bottom of her heart, she appreciated Kim's toughness and acting as her accountability partner.

It was a sunny day, and Kathy and Kim were going to meet. Kathy bought a bunch of flowers to give to Kim to show her appreciation. When she told Kim that her health was back to normal, Kim's eyes filled with tears and she said, "Yes!"

Raise your intelligence

Besides the strategies discussed so far, have you ever thought that you could improve your own intelligence? Improve your own sixth sense for studying so that you could exchange the information between your mind and outside resources? Have you thought about improving your hunch so you always get it, get it, and get it?

Where do the hunches come from? They could come from creative imagination, friendship, or love.

When a student studies with another of the opposite sex, he/she may have a stronger desire to speak with that student if he/she finds the student physically attractive. As they communicate, fondness may grow and a friendship may result. When emotion is added to liking the other person, a student's mind may become more open to possibilities—their finite thinking is supplanted by their "infinite" intelligence, because their minds have been stimulated. Under such a circumstance, a normal student can become a genius student. Students' energy can become higher under the influence of students of the opposite sex.

David was a below-average high school student. His attitude was laidback, and he never finished homework on time. When his mother checked up on his academic progress, he felt like she was nagging; she stressed him out. Her anger over his low grades was evident. Finally, she was stressed too because she worried he would not be admitted to any universities. David's mother hired a tutor, a first-year university student named Jennifer. Jennifer had long, curly hair, was very tall, and came from a European family. She smiled so much, people often believed she had nothing to worry about and that she was the luckiest girl in the world.

Not even two tutoring sessions had passed, and David had changed his attitude toward studying. He became focused on his schoolwork; he felt that studying was an interesting thing to do. When Jennifer gave him an assignment, he always completed it on time. Occasionally, if he had some questions or did not know how to do the assignment, he was motivated to call Jennifer and ask her for help.

David arrived to his tutoring sessions fifteen minutes early and began arriving to school a bit earlier too. Also, he no longer needed his mother to remind him (or "nag" him, as he used to call it) to complete his schoolwork. David's change of heart was all due to the fact that he liked Jennifer for her positive attitude and charming personality. Simply put, he could not wait to attend his tutoring session with her.

By the end of high school, David performed well on his examination and was ranked number three in his class. He had become a confident student who quickly grasped concepts in the classroom and no longer needed to spend great amounts of time studying outside of it. He had become an academic "natural." His transformation was amazing. He even began to help other students.

It is undeniable: A positive interaction between students of the opposite sex can stimulate a student to perform well academically.

Recap
Overall, to achieve more and to complete more in less time, you will have to apply some strategies:

- Clarify what you have to do and plan
- Stick to your plan
- Have good feng-shui for where you study
- Take a nap every day
- Reward yourself often, even for small progress
- Know your big rock first, and do it first—prioritization
- Study the principle 80 percent of the time, and study the Qs & As 20 percent of the time
- Form a group to study
- Have a study buddy or accountability partner
- Raise your intelligence by socializing or studying with the opposite sex

Different people have different personalities. How you apply the strategies noted in this chapter is solely up to you. You may not use all of them, but certainly you can find one of two that are applicable to you. Once you have mastered these strategies, you are ready to make a big commitment.

Chapter 5

Commitment

What is commitment?

Commitment is a strong sense of intention or dedication to a particular cause, belief, or organization, combined with a willingness to get involved. Commitment presents itself as a serious statement of purpose or plan of action.

When we discuss commitment, the first thing that comes to mind is the outcome or result of the achievement. But in reality, commitment is like a marriage. Getting married is not the end, but the beginning of the journey. Commitment is not only the promise of a certain result, but also the tools and processes required to achieve the goal. This involves devotion of time and effort. If we make a commitment for the end result only, but don't put any effort into the process, then the commitment is only a promise of the result. This type of commitment will lead to a zero result.

Therefore, there are two important components to commitment.

1. Outcome: a momentary snapshot
2. Effort: the process of the journey of making your way to the outcome

When we commit, we make ourselves available to each of the above. For example, if your goal is to become a *New York Times* bestselling author, then you will make statements like this:

"I am Jessica, and I am committed to becoming a *New York Times* bestselling author. I commit to write five hundred words per day on my blog, read one book every two weeks, and implement two writing tips per week. I would like to achieve that goal in one year, by December 31."

Why do we need to make a commitment?

Commitment is the solid ground for any type of achievement. Without commitment, nothing can happen. Have you read *Outliers* by Malcolm Gladwell, a book I briefly touched on in Chapter 1? The secret of success is disclosed in his book. That secret is ten thousand hours. Working on any project for ten thousand hours will make you an expert. If you work forty hours a week, fifty weeks a year, then you have to work five years to become an expert in one area. Without commitment, without doing the same thing for long enough, you will not be able to produce the predicted outcome.

What is the obstacle that keeps us from committing to things?

Many people want to be successful and know that this requires commitment, so why has the commitment not yet been made? What blocks you from making it?

The number-one reason why we cannot commit is indecision. We spend lots of time comparing different choices and weighing the pros and cons, but we still cannot come to a conclusion. Over-thinking causes indecision. Here is one example:

Case study one

Student Amy asked student Steve, "Hey, Steve, what are you going to eat for lunch today?" Steve said, "Express Thai outside the campus is good, or maybe McDonald's inside the campus, or no, maybe I will go to Mexicana for burritos."

The food you eat for lunch is neither a big deal nor as complicated as rocket science. It would not cause significant health issues if you chose any of the restaurants Steve mentioned. Why can't Steve make a decision between the above three? Because every one of the restaurants to him is a maybe, not where he really wants to go. Therefore, he cannot decide. Another reason could be that the more he compares, the more confused he gets. There is no "perfect" choice; it is just a matter of one choice being better than another. If you can't make your choice in the first three seconds, then don't worry about it. You don't like any of them. Just go somewhere else.

Case study two

Realtor Christina drove her clients Tina and her husband, Michael, to find a property to lease. The couple had just sold their beautiful house and had one month to move out and get their house ready for the buyer. They saw the first condo unit; it was not big enough. So they went to the second one. They liked the size, but the layout was not good. For the third property, the size and layout were good, but there was no swimming pool. Tina wanted to swim in the pool every night after work, so the third property was not her choice. The fourth property had a swimming pool, a nice layout, and was a good size, but the building was a bit outdated. So the couple checked out a fifth property, and on and on.

One night Tina's friend Lise called and asked Tina if she and her husband had found a rental yet. They told her no and the reason why. Lise was frustrated with her friends for being so indecisive, but wanted to help them, so she created a "satisfactory" checklist:

1. Location
2. Age of the building
3. Size
4. Direction windows face
5. Layout
6. Swimming pool
7. Price
8. Granite countertop in kitchen
9. Big master bedroom
10. Big balcony

Lise asked Tina and Michael to consult the list she had created as they continued their search for a home. As long as they could check at least six of the ten listed items, Lise advised, then they should sign a lease agreement so they could move forward with their lives. With Lise's advice, Tina and her husband chose a condominium unit the very next day.

From the small things in our daily activities, we should create a habit of deciding, such as where to eat, what to do, where to go, and how to spend our time. Let decisiveness become a habit.

Sometimes, we cannot make a commitment because:

- Once we do, we may feel we have lost our freedom and have become trapped.
- Doing so will settle us, but ironically, also make us feel uncertain.
- We fear we may be making the wrong decision.

- We fear facing the consequences that we committed to.

If you have any of the above feelings with regard to a commitment, please don't move forward. The commitment should be a sweet journey, not a bitter adventure.

Once you commit, you should feel joyous about the new journey you are on. You voluntarily want to tie down yourself and your time. You want to risk all you have to achieve your goal. Therefore, commitment comes with continual effort.

Case study three

Nancy's son Bob wants to be a competitive football player. He is Asian and not tall. He joined a football team when it was suffering from a lack of players. In the beginning, the new players were not allowed to go on the field. Instead, they were asked to sit on the bench and observe. Bob did the same. Game after game, he sat there, just observing, bored to tears. As the year went by, fewer and fewer sideline teammates stood by Bob. Many of them had left. Varsity football was no longer part of their daily routine, and they wanted to spend their time somewhere else more productive. Sitting on the bench was no fun and not a good use of their time.

Bob did not fully understand their reasons for leaving, but he speculated that perhaps they felt they were not good enough to play at the varsity level. Maybe they thought that they weren't receiving enough playing time for the amount of practice they put in. They might have thought they could find a better activity.

How could a nonathletic person like Bob ever hope to have substantial playing time on the best football team in the league? Bob watched game after game, and he gradually grew interested in football. He was called by his coach to play one day after one of his teammates was injured. At that moment, Bob felt that all his waiting had paid off.

He remembered very clearly how bright the sun was that day as he wore his school's red and white.

At the moment he was called to the field, Bob had decided two things: One, he loved to play and would never let anybody take his position. Two, he wanted to become a valuable asset to his team.

After that, Bob played every game, even on special teams. He was only taken off when his team was winning by a huge margin. During every game, he looked at his teammates on the sidelines and remembered that he himself had been in the very spot they were in just two years earlier. He wanted to help them get on the field too. Through this experience he had learned that everything is possible with patience and persistence. When the opportunity arises, grab it and don't let go. Never give up on what you love to do. Bob's experience taught him great values, and he took these lessons he learned and applied them to everything he did. Bob's commitment to football made him happy, and he never felt trapped or like he had wasted his time.

The commitment that you make is the direction you choose to go. It is the destination where you want to be. So there is no need for uncertainty. It is the place you are meant to be, the place where your heart smiles. Being there, you are completely fulfilled in yourself and there is never a regret.

Case study four

Peter and Alice have known each other for two years. They feel that they are truly soul mates. If they don't see each other for a whole day, the time feels like a decade. They love each other and feel that they were born for each other.

They want to get married right away. They feel that settling down together will be great. Their commitment is on track; they are headed right to where they belong.

What is the reason that some young people do not stay true to their commitment?

Many young students have lots of dreams and make decisions to achieve certain things. But they cannot always stick to the things that they have committed to. Why?

First of all, most young people, maybe 90 percent of them, lack self-discipline. They want to do certain things, but they cannot do them on a regular basis or for a certain length of time. Why? Too many distractions. What causes the distractions? Social media is the number-one culprit. Every few seconds, friends on Facebook, LinkedIn, Twitter, YouTube, Google+, or WeChat click on something, present something interesting, a hilarious joke, or share pictures from some adventures. You hear "ding," and you want to see what's going on. Once you go there, there are so many interesting things happening that you never come back to real life. Temporarily, you choose to live in a virtual world instead of the real world. It is very easy for people to get lost in the virtual stratosphere.

How do we solve this problem?

We can find the solution in one person's entry on WeChat: "The God delegates me for this mission: must lock QQ, close Wechat, take away ipad, cut internet, break cell phone, destroy the computer, remove wi-fi, and finally make you bored. Then you can sit down, introspect, read, and become wise … Just share! Study, study, and study …" Using WeChat icons, a second person agreed but cried. A third person cried.

"I fear the day when the technology overlaps with our humanity. The world will only have a generation of idiots," Albert Einstein said. If you like, please read more: http://url.cn/NurwB0.

Nowadays, whether you are eating, staying in bed, taking a bus, sitting on the toilet, meeting with friends, or even enjoying a good time with your boyfriend/girlfriend/spouse, day and night, all the time, people are staying on the cell phone or staring at the cell phone.

Peggy McColl, from Ottawa, Canada, is writing a book called *Disconnect to Connect*. She wants people to disconnect from high-tech stuff temporarily and pay attention to the people and things around them. It's a worthwhile experiment, and one you should try. Whatever you do, it is time to gear yourself up to study more effectively.

This mission will mostly rely on you.

Of course, you can ask others to remind you as well.

Someone could help for discipline. Who could this person be? It could be:

- Your parents
- Your teacher or tutor
- Your friends at school
- Your accountability partner

How can they help you? Do they need specific knowledge? No, they don't. The only thing that they need to know is your plan of action. Be specific. You schedule a time for your specific subject or activity. Then your accountability partner follows up with you, holds you accountable, and checks how far you are getting with your work. It is a great way to monitor your progress.

Therefore, every time you fall off track, they will find you and bring you back to reality.

How do we cultivate and sustain commitment?

Commitment could be starting from zero. At zero, people have no commitment. They don't feel any desire or purpose to make any kind of commitment.

Commitment can begin to occur when people are inspired by other people they like, love, or just share common interests with. People will think that they can do the same thing when they see others doing it. At this point, people start to have some sort of idea. They start to show some interest, but may not be ready to make a commitment. They talk about it, compare different ideas, and partially get involved. During this stage, people behave more like an audience than as presenters.

As their desire grows stronger, they start to realize that this is what they truly want to do. They start to fall in love with the action, and they finally believe that this is truly important. It is crucial for them to make a decision and commit long-term. Then they start to show up, follow through, and stick with it.

How do you grow your commitment?

Commitment happens when you take time and work toward it.

Commitment grows when you feel that your goal is something that you could do to become successful.

Commitment grows when you solve a conflict or confrontation.

Commitment grows when you support one another's leadership.

Commitment grows when you play and have fun during your break time.

Commitment grows to another level when you overcome an obstacle.

Commitment grows when you have a partner and hold each other to high principles.

Commitment grows when you appreciate and respect the opportunity that you have met, and respect what you have done or achieved so far.

Commitment grows when you challenge yourself to take the next step and move forward.

Commitment grows when you build your relationship with others.

Commitment grows when you experience a victory with others.

Commitment grows when you learn from mistakes or setbacks.

Staying committed

Oops! You got D marks on your midterm exam. What are you going to do? Quit school? You believe that you cannot do it anymore. Your parents and friends are blaming you, saying how dumb you are! People are talking about you, and you don't know how to handle it. Your peers think that you are not very cool. You start to doubt yourself. But it bears repeating, as noted directly above, "Commitment grows when you learn from mistakes or setbacks." Don't let a low grade get you down; turn it into a lesson that will help you improve on the next assignment. Keep reading.

Gosh, what could you do to correct this? Could you think of a way to improve the situation? Of course you can. But how do you believe that you could improve?

The famous inventor Thomas Edison once said, "I have not failed. I've just found 10,000 ways that won't work" (http://www. brainyquote.com/quotes/authors/t/thomas_a_edison.html).

Each time a particular idea doesn't work is an opportunity for particular feedback. There is no failure, only feedback.

Each time you receive D marks, take the opportunity to find out how to improve yourself. The more dissatisfied you are with your marks, the closer you get to good marks by way of feedback and improvement.

First of all, you need to free your mind from this "failure" (not "failure," but "feedback"). Realize that this is just a temporary situation representing the current state of your study; it is not you.

Shift this negative feedback to a positive outlook. It is inevitable that everyone must face failure. Even students who get A marks have failed before. But because they failed earlier, you may never know it. Recognize that the more feedback you receive, the more success you are likely to have.

Take action to identify the root cause. Allow yourself to take a break. Do something mindless like walking a dog or taking a shower. Give yourself something simple to do so you can focus. Once you identify the problem, you can simplify it and take the first step to improve. From the first step, you build your confidence. Then you start to believe in yourself. Learn to get through the feedback, not get stuck to the feedback.

Act against your fear. Do something that you think you cannot and start your journey of self-growth.

Another way to sustain and grow your commitment is not to view the commitment as an impossible burden.

Personal interest leads to commitment. Commitment is power. Once you have commitment, every once in a while you need to come back to refine your goal and reclarify your vision. The result for your commitment comes long-term. It needs to be reviewed quarterly, monthly, weekly, and daily. It could be in the form of writing, speaking, visualization, storytelling, or in the form of drama. It is very easy for people to make a commitment, but most of them will forget their commitment after a month. They get dragged down by their daily routine and forget the long-term goal. So the commitment must be reviewed daily in order to keep it current.

How do we do that? We could do any one of the following:

- Posting a daily affirmation every day on Facebook or writing an affirmation in a notebook.
- Telling the people you see every day, in an interesting way, how they could help you celebrate if you reach your goal. This will help them cheer you to victory.
- Reminding yourself what you are supposed to do for your daily activity, weekly plan, and monthly action.
- Visualizing your goal in the form of color, place, taste, smell, and feeling.
- Connecting your daily activity, weekly plan, and monthly action by converting it into a story, drama, or song, and performing it for your family or friends regularly.

When you have reviewed your commitment, create a drama or story about it. In the drama, you will clearly define your goal and visualize it with a sixth sense. You also can designate different characters and assign them individual roles. Don't forget to assign yourself a role too. Every time you show it to other people, you also must ask yourself what you have learned from this performance. As you move your action plan forward and advance, then take your progress and re-edit your drama. The more satisfaction that you gain from your drama, the more significant you will feel and the stronger the possibility that you will stick to your commitment. Your commitment is not a burden, but a magnet that you want to stick to until the end of your journey.

In this drama, who is the director? You. Who is the producer? You. Who is the organizer? You. How can you lose the game? Impossible! You are the leader in your drama group. You lead your group with your positive attitude and action. You control the speed, pace, and rhythm for achieving your commitment. You make a plan, follow-up daily activities, and stop when the time is up.

You may ask, "Why do we need to stop, not go, go, go?" Because if you work too hard, then you get burnt out and become unhappy. Your mind will take account of this too. Your lead will slip. That's because you've made the commitment too big, a hard journey, an impossible burden. Sometimes, we need to go slow instead of going fast.

Make the commitment an easy thing; repeat similar activities every day. Just like how you can go home easily, without thinking too much about route and directions or which bus you will take.

Another way to sustain and grow commitment is to recognize the benefit of the commitment and raise it to a higher level.

After you make your commitment, figure out the advantage of reaching your goal and make the commitment become true.

What could the benefits possibly be?

- Improving yourself
- Improving the community
- Meeting and spending fun time with likeminded people
- Stretching yourself and expanding your skills through daily activity, realizing that you could do more things than you thought
- Learning how to lead
- Learning to rise above the challenge through conflict and confrontation

Once you accomplish something significant, you will need a higher standard for your commitment. After raising your commitment standard, you still want yourself to feel successful and challenged. Why is that?

A commitment has to be to something big, so that you feel successful if you achieve it, but not too big. It is normal for everyone to want to be successful. This encourages people to keep going. The victory keeps people "wanting."

A commitment has to be challenging too. If the commitment is not challenging enough, and anyone could do it easily, then you may become bored. Even though you achieve your goals, you may not feel excited. So the commitment needs to be challenging enough for you to feel excited, like you're trying something you've never tried before. Invest and develop your time, not just know and produce.

Sustain and grow your commitment through appreciation and respect

You will be interested in doing whatever you have committed to. You will feel that you are making a significant contribution. You will appreciate yourself and respect the work that you have done. This type of appreciation and respect will keep you committed to your goal.

When you are working with other people toward the same goal, give them respect and appreciation. Give them work that falls within their expertise and interest. By doing that, you make them feel that they are doing important, great things. Therefore, they are committed to the activities 100 percent.

Keep your commitment simple and important

Model commitment with respect and appreciation. Take time to think about what you have done and what other people have done. Take time to like your work and others' work. Respect and appreciate your work and others' work in a humorous way. Give recognition with gifts and celebration.

If conflict arises, keep the conflict focused on the setback itself, not the people.

Sustain and grow your commitment by listening to feedback

What is feedback? Feedback is the discussion surrounding the things that happened in the process; it could be good feedback (something is working) or it could be bad feedback (something is not working).

Being a good listener and asking yourself and others for feedback is an important part of achieving your commitment. Ask yourself to think in a different perspective, ask for different resources. The resources could be people from a different religion, different culture, different age, different career, or even people who have completely different ideas about what you are doing. Don't underestimate them; they may give you fresh, new ideas.

Listen to the issues and problems that help boost your interest and confidence to solve problems. This confidence and interest will help you think clearly and creatively. This also helps you increase the curiosity to stick to your commitment.

Sustain and grow your commitment by owning your commitment

You have made your commitment. You feel confident enough about yourself to fulfill it and achieve it. Recognize your God-given gifts and encourage yourself to try out new things. Recognize that God will give you wisdom and talent to complete your action plan. Public speaking may be what is required. The influence that you have received from other people will improve you. The ownership of the commitment helps you move forward, not go backward.

Sustain and grow your commitment by celebrating

Assign a date for celebration and recognition of each small progressive step or even setback. If you make progress, you will remember and learn how you accomplished it and how you can keep making progress in the future. If it is a setback, celebrate that too. This is hard for most people. Normally, people will feel upset about a setback. But to the contrary, every setback is a breakthrough. Every time things don't work, consider why they did not work and how could you try another way to improve them and make them work. By celebrating the setbacks, you will remember what you have learned and you will not make the same mistake again. Celebrating setbacks is part of human honesty; it is a fair way to accept who you are, accept yourself as is, and keep working. Celebrating setbacks also is a form of admitting mistakes. If people don't even admit their mistakes, then they never will improve.

Celebrating progress or setbacks allows you to recognize your commitment from zero to something, from small to big. Each time you celebrate, your vision will grow bigger; your willingness to stretch will grow bigger; and, therefore, your commitment will grow bigger too.

Celebration is a way to understand your current level of commitment. It is a way to recognize the current value of your commitment. The more you celebrate, the more interest you will grow in your commitment.

Celebration also is the yearning for the commitment. Ask yourself what the commitment is for. Ask over and over again so that you will get a clearer vision of it; you will reach a higher level of understanding. From there, you will do more to follow through on your commitment.

Chapter 6

Physical Strength

T raditionally, people think if your muscles are strong, then your brain is weak. Often people see sports as a diversion from the real business of study. People think of physical education as empty, a time waster, and a distraction for students. It seems that no one wants to make too much of an argument for sports and how sports could develop one's potential and build character.

Why? Because people believe that the more time students spend on study, the more intelligent they will become. People believe that sports is directly associated with body strength and has nothing to do with mental intelligence. Therefore, the more time students are driven to sports and taken away from study time, the less intelligent the students may become. This is a big pitfall.

In modern society, as an individual, it does not matter what you do in your career; everything you do is a competitive athletic race. Not only are you required to know the vault, but also to have muscle. Without good health, this race is not affordable for you! Sorry. The number-one asset for an individual is body strength.

Recently, I studied Howard Gardner's theories, the person who introduced the concepts of multiple intelligence and emotional intelligence (EQ). Gardner mentioned that kinesthetic intelligence is also an important intelligence factor.

The core of body-kinesthetic intelligence controls one's bodily motions and the capacity to handle objects skillfully. This type of control includes timing, a clear sense of the goal of a physical action, and the ability to respond to things.

People who have a high kinesthetic intelligence will get up and move around into a learning experience quickly. They are action-focused doers. Normally, they are good at physical activities, such as sports, dancing, acting, and making things.

Gardner believes that people who have high kinesthetic intelligence could be good musicians, actors, dancers, builders, police officers, and soldiers.

Because physical activity is so tightly connected with intelligence, being physically active is considered necessary for a high level of intelligence.

How can sports develop one's potential and build up one's character? Let us take football as an example and look at a case study.

Get up and pick yourself up

In football, when you are tackled to the ground, your body becomes numb. You are temporarily anesthetized. You feel that it would be impossible to get up. At this moment, the coach shouts, "Get up and walk it off! You will be alright." Hearing this voice, at least you realize that your ears are working. You thought that your back was broken, and you could not move. But you try a little bit with the coach's encouragement. You move your legs, realize they are good, but you fall hard. A huge pain goes through your body, even at the cellular level, to every nerve. Reluctantly, you try to move again, realize it is getting better, and with the assistance of your team members, you finally get up. This is the skill that you have had since you were little. But you almost forgot it before the coach brought it up. You can carry this "get up" skill and apply it to different areas of your future life.

For each session, sometimes you win and sometimes you lose. It is easier to deal with a win than a loss. When you win, you simply feel joyful and celebrate with laughter; you hug your team members and jump around. But when you are losing, it is hard for you to face the ongoing game. Your coach taught you, "When you are knocked down, you must learn to pick yourself up." Why? If not, you will be defeated forever. Picking yourself up is another lifetime skill to apply in other areas in the future. It teaches you how to face failure. With the skill of picking yourself up, you learn that there is no failure, only feedback. When the feedback is that something is not working, you make the correction, and do it again.

Every time you pick yourself up, you are reborn. You become a new "you," with a better mentality and spirit; you become a new "you," with better knowledge and experience. You are reborn for glory.

Community, play as a whole

This entry is from Bob's football diary.

> *This whole time I was playing for myself. It was not until the next game that I realized that I was playing for my team, my brotherhood, for the starters, and the substitutes. During the next game of our season, I was a starter, something I had never hoped I would be. Yet, I had not forgotten where I had come from. I was given the chance to play through an injury, however many of my teammates had not even played yet. I was determined to play my best in the hopes of letting them play. In the first quarter I came out slow and missed several tackles. Although my teammates told me that it was alright since it was only my second game, I knew that it was not alright to be anything less than my best. Reminded of my brothers on the sidelines I played with confidence, and as a result the other team had to punt. By the second quarter we were winning by 21 points. The coaches switched me off for the second half and had other players play. I felt elated that my brothers would feel the thrill of playing football that I had felt. They could finally use what they had learned in practice.*
>
> *Through each and every game in the season I played for my brothers, for the people that would not regularly see playing time. I played my best, when I played for them.*

People often think that the players all play for the championship. But from Bob's diary, we learn that he is playing for his brothers, the starters, and the substitutes. He plays hard and wants to win by a lot so that the coach can let the people sitting on the sidelines play for some time. Why? Does this seem stupid? No. Because the boys understand each other's feelings as starters. Many people were sitting on the bench and stayed on the sidelines for a long time. Even though they all liked football so dearly at the beginning, some of them left eventually. Sitting on the bench allures nobody! They felt that they would have better ways to spend their time. As for Bob, he had sat on the bench with his teammates for a long stretch. He had created friendships with the other boys. He got support and guidance from the boys who had better skills, and finally he got the chance to play. He wanted to play harder and win more so that his teammates could come on the field.

When team members play together, they learn from each other. They use their own personal skills and spirit to inspire and impact others. That is how they stay together, play together, and become one pack. Sometimes, they call their team "wolf pack."

They carry their pack together in the good times and the bad. Each member stands on his own position and does his own job. It does not matter whether he is a runner, receiver, blocker, or tackler. Normally the wide receiver catches the ball, holds the ball, and runs through the line. But that does not matter. This player is equally important to the other players, who create the alliance and wall of defense to prevent the opposing team from running through. The team wins through working together. Personal or individual credit is not important anymore; this is a whole team. When they win, they win together. When they lose, they lose together. Win or lose, the joy is having a lasting sense of oneness with the rest of the team.

This oneness is, as William Wordsworth says, "While with an eye made quiet by the power of harmony, and the deep power of joy, we see into the life of things" (http://www.bartleby.com/145/ww138.html). Team members who have this type of spirit see another member as "that too is me," just like great philosopher Arthur Schopenhauer said when he saw another person walk down the street. "Another" is simply an extension of oneself. With a sense of oneness, you don't have to lose yourself as an individual. To the contrary, you will ride on your ambition, your competition, and your desire for the success of the whole team and bring your fresh air and give it to the team as a whole. As such, the whole team thrives together and desires the glory together. A sense of oneness can bring a constant joy to all your actions.

Supersede oneself

Through sports, one could supersede himself. Let us read another football diary entry from Bob.

I first started playing varsity football because all of my friends were doing it. But with each successive practice I began to enjoy football more and more. I was never considered an athlete. I didn't even play sports until the ninth grade. I still remember falling twice during my very first practice, just from running. How could a nonathletic person like me ever hope to have substantial playing time on the best football team in the league? It was through working hard at each and every practice that I was able to be a person that was always on the field. I would do extra repetitions of each drill and analyze film of both our teams and theirs. I took steps to better myself as a football player.

What if you are a completely nonathletic person, but you like football very much, what do you do? If the opposite player standing in front of you is four inches taller than you, twenty pounds heavier than you, and clearly more muscular than you, what would you guess? You probably would guess that he is a better player than you. He may have better speed, agility, and strength. What do you do next?

A. You go back to your coach and ask to change the position that you play.
B. You quit and give up this run.
C. You pretend to defend him.
D. You square up! Forget the frame and limitations that you set for yourself. Play, and then find out what is your advantage over him.

I hope that you choose D. In life, many times, we imagine that the problem is bigger than us. We start to disbelieve ourselves and doubt ourselves. We start to have fear and cannot conduct ourselves normally. We even want to quit and try to avoid the problem. In football, whether you are bigger or smaller, when the game starts, it is time to play. You don't have much time to speculate about the possible result and decide whether you are going to play or not. There is no way that you will play or not play based on the estimated possible result. Just go ahead and play. Square up! Conquer grinding self-consciousness and bring yourself to play. The "yourself" is not the real you, but the one you bought for yourself based on the limitation and frame that you have set for yourself. Crush that "yourself," forget the limitations, the frame, and the boundaries that you set. Stand outside of the box and go for it. Believe that you are bigger than the problem. Just do it.

Sharpen your weapon

Braveness and spirit are not enough tools to become a good player. In order to become a good player, you need skills and body strength too. The skills and strength cannot be built within one day, but through the continuous training and practice. From football, like many other sports games, you could learn to sharpen your weapon. Let us see how Bob built his strength. Here is another one of his diary entries:

> *My thirst for improvement led me to find ways to develop myself as an athlete. I did hours of research online in hopes of finding the right workout and diet plan. I asked several of my coaches for drills that I could do to improve all facets of my game. At the end of all my research I came up with a workout and diet plan that would propel me to greatness.*

Weight Lifting

- *Three times a week*
- *Compound exercises only*
- *Three sets of eight reps for all exercises*
- *Dead-lifts: started at 135 pounds and moved to 200 pounds by the end of the summer*
- *Squats: started at 135 pounds and moved to 180 pounds by the end of the summer*
- *Bench press: started at 95 pounds and moved to 135 pounds by the end of the summer*
- *Overhead press: started at 45 pounds and moved to 80 pounds by the end of the summer*
- *Lat pull-downs: started at 70 pounds and moved to 110 pounds by the end of the summer*
- *Rows: started at 90 pounds and moved to 115 pounds by the end of the summer*

Agility and Speed Training

- *Twice a week*
- *Various cone drills*
- *Various agility ladder drills*

I had my diet full of healthy proteins, fats, and carbohydrates to complement the progress I was making with each workout.

Diet

- *2,700 calories*
- *180 grams of protein a day*

- *75 grams of fat a day*
- *326 grams of carbohydrates*
- *Only lean meats*
- *A protein shake after every workout*

At the end of the summer, I showed up with renewed energy. I was so ready for the upcoming season. Within a couple of days of our training camp, my coach asked, 'Bob, what did you do this summer? You look bigger.' I showed him my workout plan. I also shared the workout plan with my teammates, so that they could get a reference to develop their own.

Not everyone was born for football; not everyone has the talent on the very first day. But, fortunately, everything is a learnable skill, as long as you are teachable. From a nonathletic person to a football player, you need to work like a dog for transformation. Whether you are a runner, receiver, blocker, or tackler, you practice, practice, and practice to gain each small improvement. Practice is to show up and do the same drills day after day. Your strength, speed, and agility are getting a little bit better each time. For each tiny increment, you gain great pleasure. The growth takes time. You need to have persistence, dedication, and commitment for every endeavor, two and half hours each day, summer and winter, rain or shine. Sometimes every one becomes completely muddy, sometimes there are blue and purple bruises all over your body, even your face. Regardless of all these hardships, never give up. By just an inch, you are closer to where you want to be—a competitive player, and a glorious man. Gradually, football becomes a prototype for every endeavor in your life. You feel that you are born for pursuing your dream persistently and with dedication. You build persistence and commitment and action into your own personality.

Play for glory, play for the championship

"Every French soldier carries a marshal's baton in his knapsack," said Napoleon Bonaparte, French emperor. This statement can be paraphrased, "He is a bad soldier who doesn't dream of becoming a marshal" (http://www.bestphrase.net/quote/every-french-soldier-carries-a-marshals-baton-in-his-knapsack.html).

It is the same thing in football. Everyone is playing for the championship and the glory. The team players are playing in imitation of heroic culture, championship culture. The championship is the playing of fullness. It is the desire and the drive for victory that makes everyone play hard. To encourage the players to fight well, the coach needs to praise them constantly for each small victory. The excitement and glory will occupy their brains, even it is not playing time.

With championship spirit in mind, you could apply it in your daily assignment. For example, do affirmations with your goal every day, so that your mind can be occupied by the excitement and glory.

Previous victories are the present evidence for victory. Present victory is also the future reference for victory. Every time you feel that you cannot do something, when you feel that something is way too challenging for you, you need to step back to your previous victory and pick up your confidence. You would know that you can do it from your previous victory and championship. Football is the way to do that.

Warriors and humanity

Athletes are warriors. Athletes have passions and dreams. They play for their passion for football. At the same time, it also is true that fear is involved in football, like many other things. As mentioned in *The Magic of Thinking Big*, by David J. Schwartz, the number-one way to overcome fear is to take action and do it. It is fear that cultivates the players' ability to go mad. It is fear that makes the players unstoppable. The moment could be very intensive and even brutal. Football unleashes the potential power of the athletes and modulates their passions. The players become fearless and dedicated; they move forward headfirst. Sometimes, there seems to be a lack of control, an abnormal craziness. This sounds crazy, but it is not. Think about if your team is in the losing position—are you still acting normally? You must become abnormal to catch up. Sometimes looking good and being normal does not work. It is the craziness that drives football to speed and ferocity. Therefore, football develops one's full potential to peak.

Even with the warriors' principle as players, they also have a human side. Every play should be following the rules of the game. Despite the fact of being on complete opposite parties, despite the fact that every party wants to be the champion, the players have to balance championship and friendship because only one party can be the champion. Some players believe that friendship comes first and competition comes second; others believe that competition comes before friendship. No matter what they are thinking, before they start the game, the players on both teams shake hands. At the end of the game, the players shake hands again. That means friendship.

US President Franklin D. Roosevelt said, "Competition has been shown to be useful up to a certain point and no further, but cooperation, which is the thing we must strive for today, begins where competition leaves off" (http://www.brainyquote.com/quotes/keywords/competition.html).

With the goal of championship in mind, the players also have the thoughts and feelings of mankind. The humanity of the players reveals their gentleness. None of the players speaks ill of an opponent, they never complain, and never whine. If the referee makes a mistake, then no one stops playing because of it. They compromise the fact and keep going.

With humanity in mind, sometimes (not all the time) football makes players well-rounded citizens.

Sometimes football teams play for a cause. They use a competition to help fund raise. This also shows the civilization of the republic. They find a way to make the drive for glory subordinate to reason. This also is a part of humanity.

Football and greatness

Football is a game that develops one's coherent, flexible internal structure. Football builds body muscle, strengthens mentality, creates a more resilient will, impacts confidence, stimulates bravery, and foments daring. Football also trains one's problem-solving capabilities. All these could benefit a post-football life greatly.

How can football develop one's greatness? From each defeat, the players learn to get up, sharpen their skills and strength, and do it again. From each play, the players learn to cooperate with others as well as learn how to become better players. From each win and loss, the players learn to excite themselves and play in fullness with glory. From each play, the players also learn to become warriors as well as good citizens.

Let's keep reading Bob's diary:

It was during a road trip game in Ottawa that I played my best. When we arrived at Carleton University, there were close to 200 people there to watch the football game. It was their homecoming weekend and all of their alumni and student body were there. I remember the excitement I felt as I got onto the field. Blood surged through my veins as I warmed up for the game. For the first time ever, I wasn't nervous about the upcoming game, I was ready for my chance to shine. Our defense started off the game, and we started off with speed, power, and enthusiasm. We forced them to punt the ball after just three downs. I had perfect coverage and didn't allow my receiver any room to catch the ball. During that game, I also made six tackles. I made no mental errors and didn't miss any of my assignments. My coaches and teammates congratulated me with 'good job' and 'great game' for my performance.

I was amazed at my development over two years. I have transformed from a nonathletic slug, to playing a perfect game on the field. If you had told me that I would play a perfect game at the beginning of the year, I would have told you, 'You're absolutely out of your mind.' Yet, it doesn't seem too crazy anymore. I guess you never know unless you try.

Football teaches people transformation. Football teaches people to work through their doubt and disbelief, which requires commitment. The conclusion that Bob came to is, "You never know unless you try." In his evolution from a nonathletic person to a team player in a famous high school league, he had to overcome his doubt. He decided to try it out because, "There is nothing to lose." Then, after sitting on the bench for a long time, seeing other friends quitting the team, he decided to stay. He wanted to give the coach a good reason to let him be on the field. With the support and guidance he got from his teammates and coach, he practiced and practiced. It was much more difficult than he thought it would be. Finally, he got a chance when another teammate got injured. He took that chance and played hard. From there, his thirst for improvement led him to invent his own workout, diet, and training plans in order to increase his strength, speed, and agility. He finally could show his capability. Now, he is a good player on the team.

Football taught him that nothing is impossible.

Interpersonal and intrapersonal

It has been said by Sun Tzu that if you know your enemies and know yourself, you will be winning in a hundred battles; if you do not know your enemies, but do know yourself, you will win one and lose one; if you do not know your enemies nor yourself, you will be imperiled

Physical Strength | 93

in every single battle. In the first five minutes of the game, each team conducts a quick estimation of the other team's ability and status. Are we stronger than them? Are we faster than them? Oh, maybe they are heavier than us, but . . . what can we do to surpass them? How we can discover our advantage to defeat them? When the two teams start to play, they gradually communicate with each other by their body language. They also categorize their ability and create some sort of hierarchy.

Football uses body communication to know and understand the other party. Football cultivates interpersonal skills. Players with high interpersonal intelligence are not only sensitive to the other players' moods, temperaments, motivations, and directions of play, but they also can react quickly to adapt to changes as they occur. With silence, their bodies communicate and respond with interpersonal skills. Sometimes, one athlete could mislead an opposing player by faking a play. This requires a high level of interpersonal intelligence. Interpersonal communication by body language depends on the leader and follower being on the same page, negotiating with each other through their physical reactions.

This is why football builds character. People who have high interpersonal intelligence are good salespeople, politicians, managers, teachers, counselors, and social workers. So if you play football well, then you can be great at any of these careers in the future.

Football is about teamwork. Each individual has to know his position. Each player has his own role in the game. Each player has his own designated work to do. But from time to time, the role also can change. The hierarchy is constantly shifting. The player knows which players he is better than and which players are better than him. Therefore, he acts his own part. Every player stands on his own position.

On the other hand, this hierarchy is not for forever. Each player has his own goal. Each player has his own desire for ascendency. Therefore, each player is working to rise. The joy lies not in who you are, but who you can be.

In this sense, football also cultivates intrapersonal intelligence. Intrapersonal intelligence has to do with introspective and self-reflective capacities. Through intrapersonal intelligence, the player has a deep understanding of himself, his strengths, weaknesses, and ability to predict his own reactions in the game.

Even though this analysis is based on football, it applies to all team sports. Sports greatly cultivate one's character. Sports are part of one's intelligence development.

In sports, students learn how to face being knocked down and get up; how to play each game as a whole; how to break the limitation that the students set for themselves, and ascend to new goals; how to sharpen their weapon by tireless practice and analysis; how to carry the championship spirit by encouraging themselves; how to become warriors as well as good people; finally, they learn how to evaluate themselves and cooperate with others.

Through each play, students train their minds. Once they have the right mindset, they have the right attitude. With the right attitude they establish good habits, and good habits build strong character and personality. With strong character and personality, they can change their lives very positively. They are ready to become great.

Chapter 7

Fun Leads
to Creativity

I f you are talking about a project, business, or your job all the time, then you are boring . . . you are extremely boring. Your business and project may suffer simply because you are not interesting or charismatic. You must have fun and add spice into your life. Life is like a drama, so you need to create a show. Do role-play rather than reading scripts all the time. You must have fun. Why? Fun builds creativity. Creativity is a major factor for human success and happiness.

Fun, by definition, is enjoyment, amusement, or lighthearted pleasure. The experience of fun is often unexpected, informal, or seemingly purposeless. Fun can be an enjoyable distraction, diverting the mind and body from a serious task or contributing an extra dimension to it. Being playful, spontaneous, and creative is crucial to fun. One may encounter fun during work, social functions, activities, or study. Normally, there is not too much logic involved.

But in real life, however, there are not many things that drive us to have fun automatically. Fun could be seeing things in a different way— more specifically, in an optimistic way. Your attitude toward things converts them into fun.

An investor for years, I have completed a number of negotiations, including ones with tenants not paying rent. These situations have sometimes led to court, judgment, and eviction. But every time I do this, I tell myself to do it in a human way, even a fun way, even though the entire situation can be very stressful. Many times, tenants have thrown me to the curb. But I try to understand that I will learn more from a bad experience. So I treat every step as a fun activity. I tell myself to complete the whole game every time I buy an investment property. Games are fun.

One time we went to check an apartment building. After the property manager showed us a couple of units, I realized that there was too much work to do in this building. Additionally, two or three units were vacant, so marketing was required as well. A friend of mine called me and asked what I was doing. I told him that I was having fun, because I thought that knowing a building inside and out was fun.

Offer surprises to others

If you can think of surprises to bring to your work every day, you already have been successful. By offering other people a surprise you give them a turning point in real life. You could deliver it in the form of shock, comedic delight, or physical human prowess. This creates great value with your creative spirit. Your surprise gives others lots of enjoyment without their expectation. Even though no one asked you to do it, this little extra will allow you to stand out from the group.

People will like you and remember you, just because you gave them good feelings and made their day delightful.

The surprise does not have to be a fun or terrifying story you've invented. It could be a different gesture that you invented today, a new naughty word, or your little brother's pee-pee story.

Surprise can bring delight or joy to someone's day. Surprising others is like adding spice to your food, making your food tastier. Surprise makes your day tastier too.

Sometimes surprising others requires lots of risk. People may have a different understanding of the jokes you told or the surprises you planned. Therefore, you may think that it is better to have a safe method of expression. However, safety kills your creativity. Trying not to look stupid often can make you look like a fool. If you don't even try, then you won't know which surprise will work and which one will not. Sometimes, after you spent time creating your surprise and sharing it with others, you can tell from their expression or body language that you made a wrong movie. Disappointment is totally okay. You find out where you went wrong, and you start something new. Each time you are cultivating your technique, you are getting better at surprising other people.

Keep working on your surprises, and you will become an interesting person. Then you can be surprised at how much other people can enjoy your creative spirit and how they appreciate your effort.

Many people think that it is hard to be creative, that one must be a genius or a natural actor or animator. But this is not true; creativity originates from the needs of reality. The first thing you have to decide is what brings you happiness. Who are you? What do you want to do? What makes you the most happy?

Just listening to your professor and completing your assignment on time is not good enough. You must discover your true self and feel your true desires. It is the strength of burning desire that allows you to bring bold questions to the table. From there, you create the solution to satisfy yourself. Wanting to become a true self is the power that drives you to create.

Then you can communicate honestly with the world how you understand it. That is your message.

Creation is not only from a fantasy or daydream, but it also is firmly grounded in reality. Standing on the reality of true observed needs, the perspective of creation gives birth.

Creativity normally comes from real-life needs. These needs could be a challenging situation or a desired situation. Need is the motivation that drives you to creation. Creativity, like many other skills, is learnable.

Creativity can be learned through training. People often think the purpose of education is getting high marks and finding a good job. In modern society, as this book has mentioned before, that is not good enough at all. Because the world is changing so fast, students must be trained to be teachable and adaptable. Many industries that are perfectly thriving today may face bankruptcy tomorrow. Take the example of BlackBerry. Let's look again at that Associated Press article, mentioned previously in this book, which appeared in the *Toronto Star* on September 20, 2013. According to the article, competition from the Apple iPhone and from Android brands like Samsung ended BlackBerry's reign as the supreme seller of smartphones—and in an amazingly short amount of time. The article further stated that the new business outlook raised the question whether BlackBerry, "once Canada's most valuable company with a market value of $83 billion in June 2008," can even continue (www.thestar.com/business/2013/09/20/blackberry_shares_halted_pending_news.html).

Here is another case study. In May 2012, Vale Inco planned to invest $2 billion toward clean air emission (mainly for sulfur dioxide). They contracted the project to SNC-Lavalin, a leading international engineering and construction firm and a major player in the ownership of infrastructure, founded in 1911. In the fall of 2012, the metal price went down worldwide. There are several reasons, one of which is the birth of nickel pig iron (NPI). Many Asian countries use nickel substitutes like NPI instead of pure nickel. The market is changing, so Vale Inco decided to reduce its investment from $2 billion to $1 billion. In the beginning of 2013, the metal price kept going lower, so Vale Inco decided to cancel the whole project to nearly zero.

The world is changing, so companies are urged to make steps to adapt. Every company or individual must be realistic; otherwise, they will be written off in the history books.

The purpose of education is to teach young people how to adapt to world change. This means young people must completely immerse themselves into new inventions. They must be able to present a fresh, unexpected way of doing things to adapt to change. New problems need new solutions! Young people must be willing to offer solutions without being afraid of making mistakes. This develops the ability to adapt. This also unleashes built-in capacity for creativity. Overall, to adapt to the new world, students need to be creative.

Knowledge or ability, natural or learned

A student may feel competent to calculate some math, do a lab for physics according to Newton's Laws of Motion, or finish reading pages one through 100. As long as he spends enough time on homework, it will be done. But if a student is asked to create, he may feel that this is much more difficult and have no clue how to begin.

To build something from nothing, you need to have creativity. Students often believe that it is hard to be creative. But often we forget that we as human beings are creative creatures. How are we creative? As God creates us, he gives us each different talents and wisdom. Humans, like many other animals, have the natural ability and learned skills to survive and prosper. Birds know to fly to their warm place in the winter, a cat knows how to capture a rat for food, an ant knows to deposit food for winter, and so on. These are natural skills. If animals have natural skills, then human beings surely have them too. Everyone is gifted with different talents. You must recognize yours. You may be good at writing: You can create a book or story. You may be good at singing: You can create a show for other people. You may be good at action: Then you are naturally talented as a sportsman. Or you may be sensitive to numbers: You are gifted as an accountant.

Sometimes, you are not born with these talents or skills. They are produced through work and experience; this is called knowledge and expertise. Learn what you are doing, do what you are doing, accumulate your experience to a certain level, and then you become an expert. Therefore, you become more creative in this particular area than other people.

You need to use tools or technology to become creative. In order to adapt, you need to use new advances to control your environment. The tools and technology could be integrated chips, Java, C++, Programmable Logic Controller, sensors, or mechanical or metal devices. These tools and technology help students design new solutions to solve problems. They also allow students to innovate new ways for the world. The students may need to work a long time to attain the expected results. That is how inventions are created.

Creativity originates from chaos

Chaos is the state of disorder. Chaos is raw energy awaiting direction. In real life, chaos can be very challenging and scary. Our purpose is to find a way to stop the chaos as quickly as possible. Even if chaos lasts just for a few seconds, people endure it as if it were hours or centuries. The amount of hardship and uncertainty within chaos causes people great discomfort. Sometimes it is intolerable. They can't stand still, constantly fighting the impulse to put the chaos in order. People communicate with their verbal language and body language. They nearly explode with ideas, opinions, and panicked cries for order. From the panic comes a wellspring of deeply felt emotion and profound ideas for change.

Most projects start with a wave of careful planning and preparation. Then comes a lot of hearty effort. The test comes when the project, along with the elements that once were carefully in place, all of a sudden erodes into disarray. Life is all about managing chaos. How you deal with the chaos in the middle of the disarray sets you apart from others.

The following is a diary entry Bob wrote after he performed in the Olympic Village with his team.

For an instant, I froze. I looked around. All the boys in my section, looking for direction, had turned to me. The only sound was the whooshing of the wind, as the pages of my music rustled and floated away uncontrollably. Another several thousand pairs of eyes were trained on our group—the SAC Wind Ensemble—we were performing at the London Olympics.

It was the kind of performance opportunity that I'd dreamed of for years—the Olympics! And here we were, jetlagged, sluggish, and now the wind was carrying away our music. I felt a moment of panic.

In that moment of consternation, I was transported back to the seventh grade, when I had a similar sense of panic. I remembered how overwhelmed I felt, looking around the room full of instruments, searching for one I could call my own. A giant brass horn caught my eye—the tuba, the one nobody wanted.

I thought I wouldn't be good at the tuba, but my teacher saw potential in me.

I started clumsily, rarely hitting the right notes. The instrument required so much air that I could only play for a couple of seconds before I was gasping for breath. I was discouraged.

But over the next two years, I was determined to defeat this elephantine monster. As I watched others hold their flutes and clarinets so mildly, I struggled to carry the bulky tuba home each day through harsh bouts of rain and snow. I practiced until my lips were rubbery, resembling weathered truck tires. The creation of complex pieces of music from each of our simple parts was my motivation to practice.

I developed a love for music and almost unexpectedly, playing became easy to me. The high notes, the low notes, and everything in between were within my grasp. I could play for an entire minute without running out of breath.

Something quite surprising happened during one of our rehearsals. Our conductor told us that we were being considered to play at the London Olympics. It didn't become a reality until our performance at MusicFest nationals in Ottawa, where we wowed the adjudicators, and the call of duty came. As our performance neared, we discovered that our section leader wouldn't be able to go. However, my peers could sense my passion and dedication for music. They naturally gravitated toward me. Suddenly, everyone was depending on me to lead them. I was nervous, but I taught my section how to play a supporting role, play in tune, and count the beat. We became better—good even!

Coupled with Ms. Chasson's conducting, I felt we were worthy of taking the international stage.

So, as we gathered for our performance on Oxford Street for the Olympics, the thousands of tourists did not unnerve me, but the wind did. The old European architecture contrasting with the modern glass buildings created a celebration of the past and future. That wind soon became an issue as it swept away our sheet music. We were lost momentarily; we rushed to pick up their music, but there was no regrouping with all those eyes on us. Thousands of people, from every country and from every walk of life, had come to listen to us play. I regained my confidence, and it was only seconds before I exchanged a glance with our conductor and started to play loudly and confidently. Soon, everyone began to follow, and then, we were back together. The tourists nodded appreciatively. The sun was shining overhead, the grass was lush, and the music flowed. A feeling of immense pride encompassed me.

As we watched the games that evening, I marveled at the magnitude of the Olympics and that I was able to contribute in my own small way. I felt, whether rightfully or wrongfully, as much a part of the Olympics as any athlete.

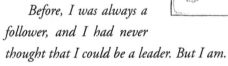

Before, I was always a follower, and I had never thought that I could be a leader. But I am.

From there, I became middle school captain and organized activities for the younger grade students. I supervised them in the morning, and at break time and lunchtime for their games. There were a couple of challenging times, but I solved the problems with confidence.

I earned the respect and trust of my peers and was elected a school prefect. I was a role model for my bandsmen. Now 600 boys look up to me. I am excited about my new responsibilities.

In this story, Bob and his band mates prepared everything well; but they could not anticipate that the section leader would find out he was not able to come just a few days before the trip. They also did not plan for the wind to carry their sheet music away. Even with these circumstances, Bob and his group must have appreciated the chaos. It is the chaos that forms the soul and opportunity. Chaos created the moment that Bob learned to stand up bravely, take responsibility, and become a leader. It was not the chaos, but his reaction to the chaos, that converted him into a leader. Even though what he tried to do may have been a great risk, which could have gone badly, it ended well.

He has learned to embrace the chaos, so he can welcome it the next time it comes.

Creativity comes from curiosity

Ivy League universities are many students' dream schools. What type of students are they looking for? Most of them will tell you that they are looking for students who have lots of curiosity and ask bold questions.

Curiosity is the number-one character trait for creative people.

When the day starts, ask yourself why the sun comes up from the east and goes down in the west. When the night comes, ask yourself why there are so many stars in the sky. How many planets are among them? Are there any human beings or other creatures on the other planets?

When you drink water from the fountain in the middle of your class session, you taste that the water is sweet. Do you ever consider that tap water may have a better quality than bottled water?

Why are the leaves of plants green, not yellow or red?

Why do we have five fingers on each hand and foot? And why do different animals have different numbers of digits on their hands and feet?

Newton wondered why the apple falls onto the ground and does not fly over the sky. That led him to find the law of universal gravitation.

Young people are interested in everything. They can ask as many questions as they like or can think of.

"One must cultivate lots of curiosity about lots of things, and then bring that knowledge to one's very specialized chosen field of focus," wrote Don Hahn, the producer of *The Lion King*, in *Brain Storm: Unleashing Your Creative Self*. Questions lead us to think and seek solutions. Let us check an essay from a twelfth-grade student.

"No change!" It was my third trip back to the car, and I was tired of returning to feed the meter; this time, I didn't have the change I needed. I didn't have the time to get it either, so I left the meter unpaid. When I returned, I had received a ticket—a fine—which was totally not fine! I knew I was not the only one plagued by the meter maid's wrath. As I talked to others, I found many people had the same problems. They either overpaid or underpaid for their parking. Some even had their cars towed after exceeding the time limit.

I began to brainstorm ideas. I asked myself, "What if there were no more parking meters, no more coins, no more going back to feed the parking meters?" In the midst of our busy lives, we should not worry about trivial tasks like parking. I wanted to remove the burden of paying at the meter, so people can focus on more important matters.

Fueled by my imagination, I started on the execution. I would use sensory technology to detect a car's position, and a mobile application for timing, billing, and notifying users when their time is near expiration.

The new system that I envisioned would allow payments to be automated wirelessly. People would not need to go to the meter to pay anymore, they would simply park their car and the device would begin to record the time that they would be parking. When they have left the parking spot and driven away, the device would stop recording and would bill them for the amount of time that they were parked. Therefore, they would only pay for the time that they parked, nothing more, and nothing less.

Having developed a blueprint for the project, the first step was to recruit partners. I pitched my idea to my friends, to no avail. None of them saw the value of my venture, but I was not going to let this opportunity go to waste. I began to ask people I did not know, and then I found somebody willing to join me, Scott. However, even with Scott's help, we still badly needed another partner in order to move the project along. I scoured other schools and it was through the recommendations of others that I met the final member of our group, Richard. His skill in computer science and his optimism made him a perfect addition. We were working together to revolutionize how we park. That's right: how we park.

We have conducted hours of market and industry research. There was no such product available in North America. With more than 10 million vehicles registered in Ontario, Canada, alone, the market is huge. After countless experiments, we built an automated parking device by using DSP chips, infrared rangefinders, and transponders. The device had optimal and accurate spatial measurement and high performance computing. With its cloud capabilities, we could store the user's personal information and bill the user through email.

We have built an Apple version for the mobile application and are creating an Android version. Both applications monitor the parking time, bill the user, and notify the user as the time nears expiration.

As a startup, we needed funding to mass produce our devices. We have written a business plan and contacted various organizations: the Innovation Initiative Co-operative Inc., Canada's Centre for Small Business Financing, and the MaRS Discovery District. They were all very interested in our project, and we have scheduled meetings to discuss funding; we may obtain a combination of loans and grant funding of up to $500,000 from these sources. In addition, I have discussed our product with several local investors whom I met through an entrepreneurship fair at my school. They have provided me with useful feedback, and with their positive reviews, we are excited to pursue this invention.

Although the project was not as easy as I thought it would be, I have learned a lot through the process. I want to use my knowledge to solve real life problems and serve other people's needs.

This business venture invigorated me to apply to Harvard University. I was attracted by the cutting-edge research opportunities at Harvard. I wanted to participate in the Undergraduate Research Initiatives. I see myself in the Program for Research in Markets and Organizations (PRIMO), and learning from the world-class faculty at the Harvard Business School. I would like to learn business strategies through social media and innovation management. By using what I will learn from PRIMO, I could make my invention a reality. I want to launch a large-scale production and monetize my invention. The only way that I could serve more drivers and parking facilities is to provide a quality product at a minimal cost. Aside from academics, I would love to meet, share ideas, and collaborate

*with likeminded individuals. Harvard is the magic place where my
dream can come true.*

Instead of studying passively, students can discover the world by
asking lots of questions. From what they learn in school or from other
resources, they can seek to answer their questions. This is how inventions
become reality—inspire students, foster their curiosity, and develop
their interest in research.

Creativity from what you have experienced

It could be from observation: the things that you saw, smelled, and
tasted. It also could be the sweet memories you have experienced or the
horrible ones. Sometimes, it could be from a habit that you have had
since you were young.

After rushing into different places one morning, I was very tired.
Finally, I landed in a Chapters store in Mississauga. I did not feel hungry,
but I wanted to order something. Yes! My favorite chai tea latté and
butter croissant. The croissant is lightly sweet, and I love it. I needed it
after the stress I felt from dealing with others' problems.

Sitting in front of the tea table, I took a sip of latté. I felt relaxed.
Gradually, my mind became vivid, my body became warm, and my
spirit began to soar. "I could create something right now," I whispered
to myself.

It was the taste of latté that comforted
me, the light, sweet taste that released me
from all the stress and anxiety. It was not
only the sweet sensation on my tongue, but
the latté also reminded me of good times in
the loving company of my mother. This is the
specific taste that I had on the day I was born.
Breast milk represents love from my mother.

I felt that I went back to Mom's arms, resting on her shoulders. What a relief! The memory has not changed for many years. I was amazed at what a small cup of latté did for me.

The croissant, small and crispy, brought back feelings of victory from my childhood. I grew up in a small rural village. Back then, there was little rice to eat, which was very rare. Because many families did not have wheat flour, they ate corn for the whole year. My grandfather was one of the richest people in the village. Many times we would eat a whole goat and half a pig. Sometimes we would have beef and horse meat. I loved cakes. I could find a piece of cake with many layers, well-cooked and delicious, in my kitchen almost every day. For other people, that was a luxury. Every time I ate a piece of cake, I felt proud. It was my grandfather who made our life much better than our neighbors'. To me, that piece of cake was more than just cake; it was filled with dignity, victory, and pride. The cake became a symbol. It was full of the spirit of my grandfather's hard work and intelligence. It was a symbol of how my grandfather challenged hard times and defeated poverty. Every time I ate a piece of cake, my heritage and my grandfather's genes filled me with confidence, and I would say, "I can do it."

So what are your latté and your croissant? Different people may have different food or drinks that wake them up, cheer them up, or bring them a spirit of creativity. Drink your latté and eat your croissant, feel your experience of love, relief,  pride, and victory. Allow good feelings to flow through each nerve of your body; bring yourself back to life and reality. So now you can create.

Creativity comes from dreaming and imagination and desire

Everything is created twice: first mentally, then physically.

How are things created mentally? Ask yourself what you want. Ask yourself why you want it. It sounds boring, but it is necessary for you to put what you want into writing and cite ten reasons why you want it every day. *Ten reasons? Are you crazy?* Yes, you must be crazy about your goal. Your ambition must be so big that you could not live without it happening physically. Your desire for your dream must be sizzling hot. Your belief must be so real that it becomes unshakable. You dream it every day. In your dreams, you have already seen it, heard it, smelled it, tasted it, and felt it. It becomes real naturally. You feel joyful, grateful, enthusiastic, and energized for what has happened. You are vibrating because your dream happened for you; it became a reality. You are constantly sending out electromagnetic waves that tell the world your good news. The electromagnetic waves create an even stronger magnetic field, compounding even bigger every time it receives more signals, and attracting good things that have the same frequency coming back to you automatically. You become more successful. You cannot believe it. It happens to you automatically. You feel so good about it that you want to take a big leap, a massive action to accelerate your success. You are very surprised by how much fun it brings you.

> *"Whatever the mind of man can conceive and believe, it can achieve."*
> **—Napoleon Hill**

Schedule your grace period

In the high school and university, many students gain the graduation certificate by acquiring enough credit scores. So their course selection is like ordering from a restaurant menu.

Appetite: All the courses in the first term are appetites. Principal: not too big, otherwise you won't have enough room for the main meal.

Main course: Main courses are the courses that you must complete in order to get the degree. Must chew slowly and go deep.

Side dish: Side dishes are the electives, the courses that resonate with you the most. Explore yourself and the world.

Soup: Soup has the nutrients necessary for your body and brain. Soup courses could be music, band, sports teams, or religious groups.

Salad: Salad is the food that supports the main course. For example, writing, debating, reading, or studying abroad.

Dessert: Painting club, swimming club, hiking club, drama club— it could be a *Finding Nemo* club too.

On campus, most students are too busy to complete what's on their plates. They try to complete various assignments and projects. They follow the professors' advice and try to get things done before the deadline. These daily tasks become a routine. If the students are bound to the routine by using 100 percent of their time, they will kill their creative spirit, leaving a spiritual bankruptcy.

Many students are barely surviving the long days, hardly getting any sleep; how could they possibly think creatively? We need to have balance. What is the balance? The balance is between existing and thriving, between what you complete and what you create, between how you enjoy the journey and the rush to a successful ending.

Therefore, you need to schedule a *grace period*. A grace period is non-negotiable. Grace period gives you time for meditation; it helps your stomach to digest what you had. If you keep yourself busy, go, go, and go, and make yourself a working machine, then you cannot have creativity and imagination. Just like an elastic ring, if you stretch yourself too much you cannot come back, and you won't have the heart for creativity. You must have thirty minutes to two hours per day for doing nothing except fun things. This is how you schedule time for thinking.

Your grace period is the time for you to digest what you have  learned. It is the time for your brain to relax for retaining and storing what you have learned.

More importantly, it is the time for you to connect with your inner child.

Allow yourself to be playful, to be curious, to imagine, or to daydream. Play and fun bring your imagination to the surface and allow your true self to shine, to live rather than just exist.

Let fun become part of your daily journey, so that you can create.

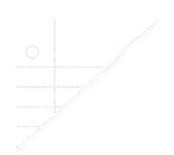

Chapter 8

The Scope
of People

What is the scope of people? According to the dictionary, scope is "the extent of the area or subject matter that something deals with or to which it is relevant." If the subject is related to people, then the scope could be you, your parents, your relatives, your friends, acquaintances, or people around the world.

In the classroom, a professor interviewed a student. He was asked what he was going to do after graduation. He said that he would find a job, a good one, because he wanted to make a good income. The professor then asked him why. The student said that he wanted to have a family. He also said he wanted to give money to his parents if he could, because he really appreciated them for supporting him for so many years. The professor was very impressed. There are not many young people who think about parents after they grow up, especially after they get married and have their own children and get busy with their own lives.

The professor then asked, "What is next?" The student said that he was going to try his best to improve his project because he was very interested in his major and wanted to become an expert. The professor again was impressed. This young student was very ambitious and motivated. Then the professor asked him what he would do if his project became very successful and he made lots of money because of it. Then the professor asked what he would do if he became a CEO of the company. The young fellow thought and thought, but he could not come up with anything except taking his whole family around the world. The professor stopped, disappointed. The young student was surprised; he did not know why he upset his professor. The poor student did all the programming correctly and received a grade of B in the class.

Why is this? Is the professor crazy? Let us review some facts.

One of the 100 greatest men in history is Mao Zedong of China, previously mentioned in this book. Mao was born in 1893 and died in 1976. He is recognized as a Chinese leader as well as a world leader. As the leader of a very poor country with a huge population, and with only limited rice and small guns, he won the war and became the chairman of China. He controlled China for twenty-seven years.

Everything happens for a reason. Let us study how Mao governed the country and his people. One of his sayings is:

"We should be modest and prudent, guard against arrogance and rashness, and serve the people heart and soul . . ." (Mao Tse-Tung, *Selected Works* [Oxford, England: Pergamon Press Ltd., 1965], Vol. III, p. 253).

Another of Chairman Mao's sayings:

"Our point of departure is to serve the people whole-heartedly and never for a moment divorce ourselves from the masses, to proceed in all cases from the interests of the people and not from one's self-interest or from the interests of a small group, and to identify our responsibility to the people with our responsibility to the leading organs of the party" (Mao Tse-Tung, *Selected Works* [Oxford, England: Pergamon Press Ltd., 1965], Vol. III, p. 315).

How could he govern 937 million people in China in 1976? The answer is very simple: Because he had all of the people in his heart. He put all his heart and soul into his work for his people. He also educated those who were working in government to do the same thing. His message was, "Serve people whole-heartedly and never for a moment divorce ourselves from the masses to proceed in all cases from the interests of the people, not from one's self-interest or from the interest of a small group" (Mao Tse-Tung, *Selected Works* [Oxford, England: Pergamon Press Ltd., 1965], Vol. III, p. 315). This kind of thought was popular then and continues to influence people today; these are the golden words that have spread out generation after generation.

Here's another example:

Bill Gates was born in Seattle, Washington. At an early age, his parents planned a law career for him. But starting in eighth grade, he developed a huge interest in computer programming, stemming from the General Electric computers bought by his school. He wrote his first computer program for playing games on the computer. His interest increased. Then he learned to create bugs by writing programming code so that he and his friends could get free time on the computer, which got them banned. But in the end, they offered to solve the problem in exchange for some computer time. His big curiosity led him to think more, study more, and do more. Gates went on to study the code running the entire system. He wrote computer programs for payrolls and students' schedules. Eventually he started Traf-O-Data with Paul Allen. In early 1973, his programs served the US House of Representatives.

As second-year university students, Gates and Paul Allen started Microsoft. Microsoft could provide a solution that the professor could not solve in the classroom. His solution was jointly published as a paper with Harvard computer scientist Christos Papadimitriou.

Gates kept discovering versions of computers. Finally, he quit school to start his own ventures. From there, Gates and his partners created tons of software to serve hobbyists, other companies, small offices, and families. Microsoft serves everyone who has a computer. Many people who have computers use Microsoft Windows and Microsoft Office, including Word, Excel, PowerPoint, Outlook, Publisher, and OneNote. These software programs are updated every year to adapt to new models of computer hardware. With these programs, people can easily write, enter data, manage contact information, keep accounts, and present their business plans or proposals. PowerPoint allows teachers to teach without dry-erase markers, chalk, or dust. All the teachers need to do is click the remote control. It converts people from presenters to speakers with drama, sounds, and dynamic movement.

In April 2010, Gates spoke at MIT, asking students to take on the hard problems of the world in their futures.

Gates stopped his work as CEO at Microsoft in 2000. In 2006, he announced plans to work full time at the Bill & Melinda Gates Foundation. He is a generous benefactor and has been ranked as the second most generous philanthropist in America. He and his wife have given over $28 billion to charity and plan to donate 95 percent of their wealth eventually.

Now let's look at Walmart, one of the most successful companies in the world.

In 1950, Sam Walton opened Walton's 5&10 in Bentonville, Arkansas, a city with a population of less than 3,000. The first year, his sales increased by 45 percent, with gross sales of $105,000.

The second year his sales went up another 30 percent to $140,000.

The third year, sales increased another 25 percent to $175,000. Within 30 months, he was able to repay his father-in-law's loan to him. The lease expired during his fifth year, when the business was making $250,000.

Oops! He made a mistake; he did not have a renewal clause in his first lease. So he was forced to close his business. With three children and his wife enjoying the town and the friends they had made, he did not want to relocate but could not find any location in town. He was forced to leave Bentonville.

He started the first Wal-Mart Discount City Store on July 2, 1962, in Rogers, Arkansas. Five years later, twenty-four stores were established across the state.

On October 31, 1969, Sam Walton incorporated his company as "Wal-Mart Stores, Inc."

In 1970, his company was expanded to 38 stores across the United States, with 1,500 employees and $44.2 million in sales. The company went public on the New York Stock Exchange on October 1, 1970. In 1972, Walmart became a publicly traded company. The company expanded to 125 stores, with 7,500 employees, and $340.3 million in sales by 1975. In 1987, on its 25th anniversary, Walmart expanded to 1,198 stores, with $15.9 billion in sales, and 200,000 associates. Walmart became the largest retailer in terms of revenue in 1989.

Starting in 1991, Walmart began its expansion into Mexico, Canada, South America, Europe, and Asia. Today Walmart owns 10,900 retail stores worldwide. The number of the associates is about 2.2 million. Now Walmart is the largest retailer in the world.

What is the secret? Let's find out.

When Sam Walton first started his retail store, he was new to the business. After he signed the lease, 5 percent of his gross sales were paid to the landlord. That was expensive. When he bought his store for $25,000, he found that he overpaid for that too. There was no way to go back; the only way for him was to move forward.

While he was operating his business, he did lots of research. He looked into the prices that his competitors offered for the same products. He repriced his products to match the competition's prices. He turned around and searched again for more suppliers. He wanted to find the cheapest price possible.

He took a loan from his father-in-law because the rent was so high and his profit margin was so low. His business caused him lots of stress.

Even under such pressure, he did not pocket the profit he could have made from the cheaper suppliers, but he passed the price margin on to his consumers. Instead he made his profit, not through price margin, but through business volume.

He chose to let the consumers save money first, then he made money second. He put other people in the first position. With this principle, he survived. His sales doubled in his first five years.

For many years, Walmart's slogan was "Always Low Prices. Always." In 2007, the slogan was changed to "Save Money. Live Better." Statistics from September 12, 2007, show that price reductions saved consumers $287 billion in 2006, the equivalent of $957 per person or $2,500 per household. Walmart put the customers' interest first, caring for the customers most.

Whenever I have bought something from Walmart, I have always been able to return the item without a hassle. Walmart guarantees 100 percent customer satisfaction.

Whether the customers are happy, one customer will talk to another 250 people, directly or indirectly. What are they saying? They are talking about the products and services. They are talking about product quality and price. They also are talking about the feeling they got from the retail experience—the customer service.

Put other people first, think of other people's interest, and serve them with your heart and soul; from there, you don't need to worry about whether a customer will come back to you. They always come back when they need your product and service.

> *"If you help enough people get what they want,*
> *you will get what you want."*
> **—Zig Ziglar**

How do you incorporate your scope?

Edward was a high school student. He liked to do research. He wanted to go to university for civil engineering. Whenever he had time, he would go to the library to do research. As a fifteen-year-old boy, he had a lot of curiosity. He found out that there are lots of beautiful and hilarious buildings in the world. For example,

1. The crooked house in the Rezydent shopping center in Sopot, Poland. This structure was designed by architects Szotynscy & Zaleski. The building lot is about four thousand square meters, with a large building that looks like it was painted by a crazy painter.
2. The Forest Spiral-Hundertwasser Building, designed by a Viennese artist and finalized by architect Heinz M. Springmann, is a 12-floor, residential building complex located in Darmstadt, Germany. The outside looks quite unusual, but the 105-unit apartment building's dancing outline has a good flow.
3. The Torre Galatea building in Figueres, Spain, which was named for the surrealist artist Salvador Dali's deceased wife, has giant

egg sculptures along the roofline. The building tells rich stories of art history.

4. The Basket Building is seven stories tall. It looks like a basket sitting in the park. It is Longaberger's home office in Newark, Ohio.

5. Habitat 67 is a housing complex located in Montreal, Canada. The structure was built for Expo 67, held in Montreal in 1967. The designer was Moshe Safdie.

Edward searched and searched; he wanted to design the abnormal building of the future. He went to Queen's University in Kingston, Canada, to study civil engineering. He liked the courses, got all A's, and a scholarship. But he was not happy. Why? Because his studies did not satisfy him. The good marks and scholarships did not fulfill his dream. He wanted to know the real purpose and needs for this study. The research he did taught him that all those great buildings were designed at a specific point in history to answer certain needs.

In May 2008, there was a big earthquake (magnitude 8.0) in China's Sichuan province. According to statistics, about ninety thousand people either died or went missing. Eighty percent of the buildings were destroyed. As a result, millions of homes needed to be rebuilt, because more than two million people had lost their permanent shelter. In addition, twenty-five townships had to be relocated.

Edward was in grade three university, but he felt a huge responsibility to go to China and use his knowledge to support the reconstruction. He saw many sad stories on the news about how people were saved and how they survived after the earthquake. The initial cause of hardship was the earthquake itself. People were injured as a direct result. The second cause of hardship was that the earthquake destroyed many roads. Impassable roads caused many delays in food deliveries, medical staff arrivals, and acquiring shelter materials. Because of the delays, Sichuan accumulated lots of needs in a short time. Therefore, the third cause of hardship was the urgent need for food, clothing, medicine, medical staff, and shelter. If any of these were not delivered on time, people were in peril.

The news showed how people were saved from their devastated homes and roads. Some people even had broken legs and broken arms, but no food. Edward felt a big need within himself to serve those people. Many of them were in danger.

Edward and his family discussed his dream to stop attending school so he could work in Sichuan to support the reconstruction project. His mother wanted him to finish university first and then do whatever he would like. But Edward said, "I understand that you want me to have a good education and a good life, but now is the time. Now China has needs, big needs. If homes and buildings are not built before winter comes, many people will be left in the cold. I was born in China, and I can speak both English and Mandarin. I have studied civil engineering for three years, and I have ideas about design. I believe that China needs people like me, Sichuan needs people like me, and the project needs people like me. I feel that I would be wasted if I stayed in the classroom. I feel useless if I am not helping when I see that many people are suffering. I cannot be selfish, Mom."

Through the sleepless night discussing it, Edward's mother finally became convinced that she should allow her son to go back to China. Temporarily she agreed, but she had lots of worries, as Sichuan was a dangerous place to stay for the time being. She did not want her only child to go there.

On the second day, Edward went to research how he could join the rescue team. He found out that he could go to the local Red Cross and register. However, it was a different assignment than he expected. He was assigned as a translator rather than an engineer. He was educated in China until grade seven, so his Mandarin was perfect. Even more importantly, he knew both North American and Chinese culture. So he could guide the rescue team from Canada and connect the crew with the local Chinese community.

On the third day, he went to school and talked to his professors. They agreed with him right away, but told him that he could not come back in the middle of the school term. If he was going to China, he needed to take one year off from school. He thought it over and said that would be okay.

He went to China. It was different from what he expected. He enjoyed working with his team and helped lots of people in need. From time to time, he worked on different projects, helped different communities, and moved from one location to another.

Time was flying; a year passed. One occasion he would never forget.

It was in the summer. Many people had been affected (about fifteen million) after the earthquake. Even though the Red Cross had the medication, it could not deliver it to the destination on time because of broken roads, broken bridges, broken hydro lines, and many unexpected catastrophes.

Edward was one of the people assigned to assess needs and monitor progress. Sometimes, he also helped with relief efforts, shelter reconstruction, restoration of water supplies, and preparation for preventing future disasters.

He clearly remembered encountering a woman who was twenty weeks pregnant. Ten weeks later, her situation had worsened. Doctors debated the risk of an emergency Cesarean Section; but if the operation was not performed, the risk would be even higher. The doctors performed the procedure. The mother lost lots of blood and required transfusions.

Sadly, there was not enough blood for the transfusions. The doctors searched and searched, to no avail. Their eyes begged people for help.

Edward recalled that he grew up in a small village. He remembered clearly how his father had died when he was five years old and how he and his mother had struggled through those years. Edward saw how the woman was struggling and fighting for her baby. Without too much thinking, he decided to do something.

Edward rolled up his sleeves and became a hero.

Edward underwent blood-type testing. It turned out he had the same type of blood as the ailing mother. He donated his blood, and saved the woman's life. The baby survived too, despite the fact it had weighed only five pounds at birth and doctors had thought its chances of survival were minimal.

Many days had passed after Edward donated his blood to the mother. It was noon, the sun was very high, and the day was hot and dry. There was not much food left. There were only some buns and apples in the village. Edward was the first one who was offered the buns. Edward wanted to save the food for the elderly people, but the baby boy's grandfather walked to him and gave him all he had. He said, "You gave life to my daughter-in-law and my grandchild. You are the hero. You should eat."

The grandparents of the baby boy hugged Edward. They were so moved, they cried. They thanked Edward for giving the gift of life to their family. The local community treated Edward like a hero.

Edward felt great pleasure that he could save the woman and her baby's life. Edward had received good marks for his courses, but the appreciation he received from the local people outweighed those marks. He felt that helping people in need was the sweetest thing he could do. He felt that he was now part of a local community and its people, which to him was better than any good mark in school. The joy of serving the community made him want to stay and help the people for life, so he followed his passion and became a permanent fixture in Sichuan. Edward knew if he hadn't, he would have regretted it forever.

Now the "baby" boy is a strong six-year-old.

Serve your country, serve your kindred

When you graduate, be ready to serve others, not only yourself.

If you only think of yourself, you won't go far. You must have a big scope to serve the whole of society, and the world.

Your heart is a container. Exercise the container so that it can accommodate more people. The bigger your container, the more people you will serve in the future and the more successful you will become.

But is there any proportional rate between your passion and the number of people that you serve? Not really! Why?

Having scope is not enough. You have to practice people skills, understand other people's needs, and incorporate your skills to serve those needs.

Be smart and humble

Be careful with your attitude and the way you convey your message through communication.

How can you serve other people so that your service is acceptable to them and recognizable to them? With a great attitude and communication skills. Without these attributes, your good heart still could get bad results.

Consider Peter, the top student in his class. In almost every course he gets an A. He does not need to work hard, because he is very smart. In class, he gets almost all the ideas that the teacher presents right away. He uses three hours in the evening to complete his homework. For the rest of his free time, he goes to the library to read books, gets involved in football clubs, and goes to movies with his roommate.

Peter is very kind. He wants to help other students complete their work. On Thursday, he finished his homework early and wanted to share his work with other people. So he came back to the dorm. It was dinner time, and everyone was home. Many people were complaining about the homework. They said it took too long to finish. Peter asked if they could come to his dorm room so that he could share his method with them. There were six students (all of them his neighbors) who accepted his invitation. He offered everyone seats and asked them if they would like something to drink. They said that they just wanted help with their homework.

Peter started his presentation with a big smile. He set up a small board so that he could write on it. He thought as he lectured about how much earlier he had finished his work than the others. He wondered if they were less intelligent. He shared every detail of how he did the work, pouring out all of his thoughts and research. At the end, he felt very satisfied that he could help other people.

Now he asked if there were any questions. No one answered. Silence. One minute, two minutes, three minutes had passed. Five minutes had passed. Peter was expecting that the students would ask questions so that he could help more. But, unfortunately, no one said anything. Not only no questions, but also no thanks.

PRIDE GOES BEFORE DESTRUCTION, AND A HAUGHTY SPIRIT BEFORE A FALL

Peter realized that there was something wrong, but he could not figure out what.

Why did the other students not ask any questions? Because they thought that Peter was arrogant. The other students were aware of Peter's pride, so they did not feel comfortable. They did not even care what Peter was talking about.

Peter felt very upset. He had a big heart at the beginning. Now it looked like no one wanted his help as he imagined.

When people communicate with each other, their attitude is revealed first. The attitude is more important than the knowledge, the talent, the degree, or the attributes. The attitude comes first. If you asked ten employers what the most important thing for an employee is, I bet that all of them would tell you that attitude is the number-one thing that they are looking for. Not the skills, knowledge, or experience.

The attitude of your communication is very important.

You need to be humble in order to become acceptable to other people. No matter what you do, humility is always acceptable, and humble people always get help from other people. If you are humble, it will help you be received by others.

What is humility?

If you check the dictionary, humility is defined as "a modest or low view of one's own importance; humbleness." But this interpretation is not quite right.

Humility is to have a modest view or fair estimation regarding one's own importance or rank. It is quiet, meek, and typically not self-serving. It is about being open to the possibility of improvement.

In modern society, we are busy and competitive. Everyone wants to be ahead in the line. Most people want to take advantage of the current situation and get the most out of it. It is hard to become humble, because everyone wants to look good and impress other people. Unfortunately, this does not do anything good for them.

> "A soft answer turns away wrath, but a harsh word stirs up anger."
> —Proverbs 15:1, ESV

A person who has the attitude of humility always gets help from the world, but a person who shows off stirs other people's hate. You will not get anywhere. Even if your intention is to help other people, if your attitude is not humble, then you will not be acceptable to other people in the first place, regardless of what you are trying to do.

In real life, some people practice humility the opposite way. For example, some people never accept compliments. Suppose someone says, "Oh, Michelle, you are very beautiful today." Instead of saying, "Thank you," Michelle says, "No, I am not. I actually did not sleep well last night because I worked on my homework 'til very late. I don't even feel good today." Is Michelle really practicing humility?

Humility is not downplaying yourself and making yourself worthless. Humility is receiving yourself as you are, putting other people first, and yourself second. Recognize that different people have different talents; you are just one of many. Humility is to see other people like your treasure, not your enemy or an obstacle in your way.

Because we are humble, we need to understand each other's point of view. Because we are humble, rather than stand on our own point of view, we need to elevate our thinking to consider the whole picture. Because we are humble, we also need to learn to forgive other people, to accept other people as they are.

When we are humble, the world comes to life.

We can approach other people with humility.

Arrogance is the opposite of humility. With a little bit of achievement, a person may be inclined to shout it from the rooftop. With pride, this becomes arrogance, because he thinks that he is better than everyone. He feels satisfied with his current situation. He believes he is the best. When a problem arises, he thinks that he is the only one who can handle it. He thinks no one could be better than him. This arrogant attitude blocks him from other people. No one is better than other people.

Serve people with a positive attitude and humility. If you can practice humility so that other people can accept you fully, then your service is complete and appreciated.

1. When you have done something, let the results speak for you. But avoid speaking about yourself directly, so that it doesn't sound like you are boasting about yourself or your accomplishments.
2. Use "you" instead of "I" in your speech. Put other people's problems first, yours second. The purpose of the communication is not showing how good you are, but serving other people and solving their problems.
3. Convey your message by stating the facts, not bragging.

Practicing humility is a lifelong endeavor. With humility, your service to other people is much more efficient. With humility, you gain respect from other people. It means that you have influenced other people in a silent way.

The importance of good communication skills

Having good communication skills also helps you serve other people. Some people work hard, but achieve fewer positive results. The more work they have done, the more complaints they receive. Why? Because they did not communicate with other people properly. They consistently create misunderstanding and confusion. Therefore, it does not matter what they do or how hard they try, they are always wrong.

What is communication? How do people communicate with each other? Communication works like a telephone. There are senders and receivers. The senders analyze their mind, organize their words, and convert their ideas into messages. This process is called encoding. The senders deliver their message by their way of speaking, painting, body language, writing, or through action. Once the receivers receive the pattern of delivery, they translate the message into their own understanding. This process is called decoding.

Communication requires that the senders and receivers be on the same page and share a commonality of communication. The commonality of communication could be the needs of the senders and receivers, the desires of the senders and the receivers, the perceptions of the senders and the receivers, the common knowledge of the senders and the receivers, and so on.

What happens in reality?

Did the senders deliver the messages exactly as they wanted to convey? In other words, did the senders express 100 percent of their ideas? The answer is maybe or maybe not. It is the same thing for the receivers. Did the receivers reveal the exact same messages that the senders gave? Or did the receivers understand fully what the senders delivered? The answer is maybe or maybe not.

Thus, confusion, miscommunication, and misunderstanding occur often. What happens next? Even if people do not understand each other fully, do they stop doing things until they figure it out? No, most people don't. Sometimes they don't have an opportunity to figure it out completely before they take action to move things forward. What do  people do? They do things based on what they think they understood.

Mao said, "Our duty is to hold ourselves responsible to the people. Every word, every act and every policy must conform to the people's interests, and if mistakes occur, they must be corrected—that is what being responsible to the people means" (Mao Tse-Tung, *Selected Works* [Oxford, England: Pergamon Press Ltd., 1965], Vol. IV, p. 16).

How can we communicate effectively so that the senders and the receivers understand each other fully? There are senders' responsibilities and receivers' responsibilities. Senders, you must understand your receivers first, so that you can address them according to their level of understanding, not to the level you are conveying. The second thing is to consider your receivers' interests and make sure that you are conveying content that keeps them listening. Third, check with your receivers by asking them questions after you deliver your message. If something is unclear, you must take time to explain the details. Each time, only convey one point; try not to deliver too much information to your receivers and confuse them. Finally, listen to any feedback that your receiver may give you. Not all feedback is what you want to hear. You must not take it personally. Discuss the feedback with your receiver and make sure that you remove the communication barriers between you and your receivers, so that you can keep your communication flowing smoothly.

Effective communication is a two-way process, not a one-way street. Listening is an important part for the receivers. Miscommunication is caused by lack of listening. Listen with your heart and follow with your mind what the senders are conveying. When you are a listener, your first requirement is to listen to the sender's message patiently. Try to understand what the sender is conveying; from there you can give your feedback. Without it, the sender cannot understand where you are or how you received his message.

By communicating at a higher level, you better serve other people. Communicate with humility and a positive attitude, requesting feedback. This will allow you to understand people better. You will know how to serve other people, because you have established communicative commonality between you and the people whom you are serving.

You must be a people person so you can do great things.

You must practice good communication skills so you can do great things.

Gladwell's book *Outliers*, mentioned previously, sheds light on the idea that mitigation is an important reason why airplanes crash.

"We mitigate when we're being polite, or when we're ashamed or embarrassed, or when we're being deferential to authority," Gladwell writes (p. 194). The captain and first officers have equal duties and responsibilities to operate a plane safely to its destination. But as Gladwell explains, in reality, if the first officer is the flying seat and the captain becomes the co-pilot, then the duties could be split equally. But if the captain is in the flying seat and the first officer becomes the co-pilot, then the co-pilot becomes subordinate. Why? Not because the first officer wants to be lazy, or take it easier, or doesn't want to take the responsibility. It is because the first officer often has less experience than the captain. The first officer thinks that he is the employee and the captain is the boss and that therefore, there is respect and authority in this work relationship.

When the first officer (as a co-pilot) tries to communicate with the pilot (the captain) he struggles to mitigate his speech. The officer's intention is to reduce the power, to be polite, and to respect the captain. In an airplane cockpit, the captain has worked for long hours and is exhausted. Especially in bad weather conditions, the captain does not have the luxury of time to second guess what the first officer is conveying. He does not have extra time to interpret the ambiguous messages from the officer. The first officer must be clear, short, and honestly demonstrate the current situation.

If the first officer conveys an ambiguous message, the pilot might not be aware of the dangerous situation, and the crew would not be able to prepare to save the airplane until it was too late.

Therefore, the airline company instituted a new training system—"crew resource management." The new system was designed to train the junior crew members to communicate clearly and assertively. The new system was also designed for the co-pilot to challenge the pilot if something went terribly awry. It allowed the flight crew to only speak one language and to call each other by names only, not by titles or rankings.

Therefore, the attitudes toward hierarchy and authority were avoided. Instead of training to improve airplane knowledge and flying skills, they mainly trained the crew members to improve their mental outlook and communication styles. The junior crew members were encouraged to speak up to help the captain out. With the new system, accidents were greatly reduced (pp. 194-197).

In any given situation, it is not proper to ambiguously communicate with other people. We should not tolerate it. Communicating clearly with others saves you and them lots of time. It is efficient to find ways to solve the problem or find solutions for the issues. Communicating clearly and assertively is a virtue.

Recap

- Stretch your heart, the container, so that it can accommodate more people.
- Be smart and humble, so that your service is acceptable to others. Practicing humility is a lifelong endeavor.
- Good communication skills help you serve others better. Be clear and assertive.

Conclusion

The youth are our future, and we must give them the necessary skills to become leaders of today. By doing so, we will be able to empower our children to become catalysts for a better tomorrow.

Thirteen years ago, a young immigrant family moved to Canada in search of a better life. They were just an average family. They had very few belongings and their poor English made finding a job a struggle. The parents started out as door-to-door salespersons, working ten hours a day, seven days a week, all the while raising their five-year-old son. Life was hard and times were tough, but they were happy knowing that everything they had came from their own hands. However, with those heavy work hours, they were missing out on their son's education.

They passed on the responsibility of teaching their son to his school and neglected their role in his education.

This mistake was not left unnoticed; Bob's second grade teacher called in his parents, Nancy and Jacob, for a meeting. The teacher showed the couple Bob's journal. On a blank piece of paper in a notebook, he had written, "Today." That was the only word. The teacher was upset because she had expected Bob would write something like "Today is Tuesday." Bob had had no clue what he was going to write, and he did not care. Therefore nothing motivated him to finish the assignment. The teacher then showed the couple another student's writing. This student wrote a story about her puppy. She described him as white with very soft, nice fur, and she detailed how the puppy greeted guests and connected with her family members. The teacher's eyes sprang to life when she spoke about this student's work, while disappointment played upon her face when she spoke about Bob's.

The teacher related how Bob's journal was filled with incomplete sentences and partial phrases, devoid of any emotion or care, while his classmate's journal was filled with colorful descriptions and feelings. The teacher was definitely not impressed by Bob's efforts. His parents were disappointed as well. To top it off, they were shocked. They were too busy with their jobs and hadn't paid attention to what their son was doing in school. After that incident, they began focusing on Bob's schooling and education. They wanted him to have a complete education, and they began to help him work toward that. During a piano practice with Bob, Nancy discovered that he was more likely to practice if he had a partner. He really "got into" playing the piano when Nancy sang or danced along as he hit the keyboard. She also discovered the same was true when he was performing his homework. When she acted as a study partner, Bob focused on completing his assignments, so Nancy began to study with him on a regular basis.

The lessons Nancy taught her son took root and would bear fruit for years to come. In the meantime, Nancy became even more committed to instilling these lessons in Bob, quitting her job and becoming self-employed to carefully oversee Bob's education. Because she was more available, she was also able to train Bob to expand his love for his family to the community and from his community and neighborhood to the world. Bob learned to serve a bigger audience by utilizing what he knew. Eventually, Nancy wanted Bob to become a complete, well-rounded man. For that reason, she took the initiative to place him in an all-boys boarding school, where all areas of a boy would be developed and he could become a well-rounded citizen.

At this boarding school it was obligatory to compete in two terms of sports, as well as to become a cadet and attend chapel every morning. It was simply not an ordinary place. It wasn't a nine-to-three-thirty school. Some students even stayed there until nine-thirty at night. It was the perfect place to develop Bob, not only as an academic, but also as a person. The results were astounding. Bob was able to join and play on the varsity football and rugby team without ever having played sports in his life. He made the team due to his hard work and practice.

Also, he was able to perform music in front of hundreds of people at the Olympics. Even though he was involved in music before he went to his new school, he never thought that his musical abilities would open up such a wonderful opportunity. On top of all this, the entire student body and staff elected him as a prefect. To add the cherry on top, he was accepted into the best school for hospitality in North America, the School of Hotel Administration at Cornell University. But his educational journey doesn't stop there. These lessons will continue to bear fruit in Bob for the rest of his life.

With the correct attitude and proper education, everybody can have success. That is why we need to support our youth with a complete education that covers all facets of life, so that they are able to become who they were meant to be. The potential to be great is within all of us; we just have to water and nurture it with the lessons covered in this book. You can have fun *and* get A's —and reap the rewards throughout your life.

Printed in the USA
CPSIA information can be obtained
at www.ICGtesting.com
JSHW082347140824
68134JS00020B/1924

9 781630 474744